To my parents,
with love and gratitude

ACKNOWLEDGEMENTS

THE REAL AUTHORS of this book are the women who shared from their hearts. Many roads converged to arrive at the collective wisdom conveyed within these pages. Although the stories were gathered over the past three years, in reality each message is the culmination of a lifetime of experiences. I am deeply grateful to these courageous women who entrusted me with the delivery of their messages. Their tales are told with references to time and biographical data reflecting the dates the original interviews were conducted.

Among these women, I'd like to extend special thanks to two who played a significant role in moving this book to fruition. Carla King was an inspiration as an adventurer, motorcyclist, writer and publisher. Genevieve Schmitt saw the concept as a finished product as soon as she heard about it. As experts and leaders in their respective fields, their support and encouragement were invaluable.

Special thanks go to the women who transformed my manuscript into a work of art. All were a delight to work with. Editor Alison Cunliffe's eye for detail and abilities to pare and shape, crystallized and strengthened the message. The team at 1106 Design set crystal clear expectations and delivered a high quality interior layout while providing exceptional customer service. Working from a medley of photos and a writer's ramblings, Lyn Bishop quickly turned a concept into a beautiful cover which perfectly reflects the interior energy.

Author and Toronto Star Wheels Editor Mark Richardson saw the potential early on and was instrumental in the fledgling draft reaching maturity. He generously provided insights, expertise, candid feedback and inspiration along the way. Author and publisher Max Burns mysteriously believed in my writing ability and was one of the first to take a new writer under his wing and get her started in the right direction. Writer Lorraine Sommerfeld encouraged and prompted me while the book was still in its infancy. She also gave me the opening line. Writer Adrian Blake pitched in and connected me with several key contacts.

Thank you to Jackie Quinton, Kristy McKitrick and Tricia Secretan for their critical eyes and guidance. A very special acknowledgement to the Universe for delivering Tricia to the chair beside me at an authors' night. That moment changed my life.

Linda Emblem coached me at a pivotal time and introduced me to the creative process that birthed this book. Around the same time, Stephen Walters entered my life and has ever since been a solid and generous supporter of my creative initiatives. Karen Hodgson lent her keen skills and endorsement.

Thank you to the many other friends, colleagues, clients and strangers who have extended kindness all along the way.

Finally, I have been blessed to have the influence of my Mennonite heritage and the enduring, enthusiastic and unconditional support of my parents and family, just as they have stood with me all my life.

TABLE OF CONTENTS

INTRODUCTION

"What I am looking for is not out there. It is in me."

— Deaf and blind author and activist Helen Keller

WE ARE ON A JOURNEY — a road trip — along our own path to awareness. Each one of us has been given choices on how we proceed. I think God has a sense of adventure and consider myself blessed that the motorcycle has long been an integral part of my journey. My motorcycle has carried me to people, places and experiences I would never have imagined possible. It has been my guide and has often been involved in some way when life has scheduled a lesson. I am where I am today because of the motorcycle.

Not everyone rides a motorcycle on their journey. There are many other ways to become aware of who you really are and experience all life has to offer. Some people paint, write, play music, go on retreats, meditate, travel, volunteer their time or coach sports. For me, it is the motorcycle.

How we learn to embrace and overcome challenges and reap the rewards weaves an exquisite tapestry that becomes the picture of who we are. This book is about our journey along our personal, emotional and spiritual path to enlightenment and becoming all that we are: why we're on this road trip. The stories illustrate how motorcycling allows and encourages this. If you don't relate to motorcycling, substitute what fits best for you. The message will still be clear.

At some point in our lives, we stand at a threshold we need to cross to reach our destination. This can be daunting, particularly when it is toward something non-traditional. Making the decision to cross that threshold has implications for how the rest of our life unfolds.

That threshold occurs at different periods in the life of each of us, often many times. We must look within, discover where we are and summon the limitless power that resides within us and moves us forward.

The motorcycle can transport us to awareness. Riding is a sensual, visceral, nourishing experience for body, mind and soul. It engages all our senses — sight, sound, smell, taste, touch — and our sixth sense of understanding and insight.

When I began this book, I knew only it was to be about women, motorcycling and personal power; and I would collect stories from women riders about how they discovered and used their own personal power. What difference did riding make in their lives? How did they transfer that to other areas of their lives? What difference did it make to those around them?

I hope the stories you are about to experience are even fractionally as significant to you as they were to me.

PROLOGUE

I LAY IN THE MUD AND RAIN, the front tire of the motorcycle spinning in the air beside my head. In an instant, my life had changed forever.

I had started the day as a student at an off-road training course. Even for a day of riding early in the season, the weather was miserable. It was cold and rainy, and the woods were damp.

Our path led us to lush mixed pine and hardwood forests awakening from their winter hibernation. Our every breath brought smells of spring: the moist earth, damp bark on the trees, spring flowers, extravagant new undergrowth, the proliferation of green everywhere amid the puddles along the muddy, rutted trail.

Every so often, our instructor would stop, dismount and demonstrate how to navigate a particular hazard, and then we'd try it ourselves. Challenging ourselves, learning new skills and successfully steering around, over or through obstacles was invigorating and empowering.

Noon was on us before we knew it. The final reward for a morning of accomplishments was a stimulating ride through another part of the forest on the way back to the base for lunch and a chance to warm up. I was exhilarated, but I was also recognizing the onset of fatigue as unfamiliar physical exertion and the battle with the elements extracted their price.

As I crested a hill and began to descend, I saw my instructor and Nancy, another student, already stopped at the bottom, just before a small water hazard. What I didn't see until it grabbed my front tire was a huge rut in the middle of the trail. I flew off my bike. I landed solidly on my right shoulder. I knew immediately my life had radically changed, if only because my right arm refused to move. I had yet to comprehend the magnitude of that change.

The instructor and Nancy ran up the hill to help. Someone pulled the bike off me and parked it to the side of the trail. I could see no obvious trauma and my arm didn't hurt if I stayed still, but try as I might, it wouldn't budge. I sat in the cold and rain, helpless.

My business centers on motorcycles, and it was the beginning of the season. This couldn't have happened to me. I was fifty-four years old and on my own. How would I ever manage?

I believe everyone we come into contact with has a message to share, and so it was that morning. Trying to distract me, Nancy pointed out the trilliums carpeting the woods directly in my field of vision. I had noticed the flowers, or thought I had. The symbolism didn't sink in until Nancy drew my attention to them. I had chosen the name Trillium Motorcycle Tours for my business because to me it meant springtime, growth, rebirth and hope, and it was the flower of Ontario, my home province.

I am right-handed, so everything I do involves my right arm. And on the motorcycle, the right hand controls the throttle and the front brake — moving forward, accelerating and stopping — all having to do with control and power. Even so, I was calm, partly because I was in shock and denial, but somehow I also knew a divine experience was unfolding. A course correction had just occurred and a special lesson awaited me. Now I had to discover where my power really was.

Nature is where I go to get grounded: walking along a deserted beach and marveling at the immensity of the ocean and the ceaseless cycles of the tide, or gazing at the stars and planets in an indigo sky on a cold, clear night. Most invigorating for me is a hike through a hardwood forest, and I am fortunate to have plenty of that in my backyard. I find a spiritual quality in the woods and an energy that doesn't exist anywhere else for me. But this time my motorcycle had taken me into the woods and grounded me. When I came out in the passenger seat of an ATV, my shoulder was broken and my life was about to be very different.

What followed was the darkest period of my life. I felt broken, alone and abandoned. It hurt physically, emotionally, psychologically and spiritually. I didn't know how I could ever be whole again. I tried to focus on my belief that out of the darkness comes growth. I tried to want what was to come: exploring, discovering and listening to my inner self. I knew the growth process would be immensely rewarding and meaningful, but the light seemed so far away.

As I recuperated at home in quiet emotional darkness amid spring rains, though, ideas could take root. It was time to reflect, refocus and restore direction.

This book germinated during that period. I decided I would collect stories from women who rode: stories about how they triumphed over challenges and grew. Some of the stories would be about motorcycling; others would be about how lessons learned through motorcycling had gotten the riders through challenging times.

I soon realized as well that I needed an answer to a big question in my own story. How did I get to the point in life where I had needed to be awakened at forty-eight years of age, but then still needed a spiritual wakeup call in the woods six years later?

And so this book grew.

CHAPTER I

How Motorcycling
Empowers Us

*"When I pull up on my motorcycle, there is an assumption
of 'Wow, there's a woman of strength,' even though it's not
about strength, it's about balance."*

—President and CEO Rebecca Herwick

EVER SINCE THE FIRST steam-engine motorcycle appeared in 1867, motorcycles have held a certain mystique. Not to diminish it or in any way take away from its power in symbolism and reach in metaphors, but a motorcycle is basically a piece of metal and a few other materials on two wheels. Yet it's also so much more. It's a partnership. Watching the mastery of rider over machine when they join together in perfect harmony is like observing a beautiful dance that gives birth to power, strength, balance and positive change.

The Oxford Dictionary defines power as "the ability or capacity to do something or act in a particular way." Empowerment makes someone "stronger and more confident, especially in controlling their life and claiming their rights."

We all recognize power differently and vary in our perception of how much power we have. It could take the same amount of power for one person to travel the world as it does for another to summon the courage to begin a new job. Regardless of where we stand, using our power brings us happiness and fulfillment, and a sense of accomplishment, meaning and purpose.

Often our power remains dormant or underutilized, but when we use our power, we discover more of it. So, how we manage our energy and who and what we give it to is very important. Negative thoughts and behaviors deplete us; positive actions affirm and grow our power base. And the ripple effects on others can be enormous. I had no idea my words would one day save a life. None of us do. So, it's important to act from a position of love and gratitude rather than fear and negativity. Whichever we use spreads, so why not spread goodness?

Powerful people are usually defined by status, accomplishments, titles or accumulation of material possessions. These illusions can cause us to lose sight of our own power and who we are.

How does a motorcycle acquaint us with our power?

It appeals to our basic nature, satisfies primal needs and brings out our strengths by providing the following ingredients, which are essential to the survival of our souls:

- **Adventure.** Riding calls to the unique, wild nature within each of us. Eventually, we answer that call, and then wonder why we didn't respond sooner. It brings us to who we are and our connection to all other living things, including the collective wisdom and unlimited power of the universe.

- **Connection with Spirit.** Nothing stills my mind like a motorcycle ride as I embrace the peace of the present moment, where my power and creativity reside. Riding encompasses all my senses, including the sixth one. Riding is great for clearing my mind of clutter and leaving worries and fears behind.

Any rider will tell you riding outside of urban areas is a spiritual experience. Traverse the mountains, cross the plains, pass through a forest or alongside the ocean and you can't miss the connection to the universe. All your senses are engaged. Your eyes take in the grandeur and beauty. Your ears note the wind as it rushes by, the crashing breakers or the silence. You smell the freshly cut hay, the redwood forests, lilacs in the spring. You feel temperature changes as you alter elevation or latitude, or approach water. You taste the salt air and the clover.

All that pales in comparison with how riding engages your spirit. You're enveloped in feelings of peace, euphoria and joy, all rolled into one. It brings you into the now, where nothing except the present moment matters.

- **Freedom.** Motorcycling represents freedom for many men and women. New riders get a taste of this as soon as they learn to ride and move even those first few feet under power. But initially, a rider is absorbed in learning how to operate the machine safely. Still, with proficiency, the feeling of freedom will grow.

Our life paths have no shortages of twists and turns, which is why the motorcycle is ideal to carry us symbolically to where we are going. It's flexible, versatile and when properly tuned, has more power than we'll ever need to carry both us and our loads, whether physical, emotional or spiritual. The motorcycle is up to a challenge, change and variety. And we alone control our vehicle.

- **Confidence.** Most of the women who participated in this book said they see other woman riders as the embodiment of power. Their body language exudes confidence, strength, fearlessness, independence and love of life. They have the courage to be who they are and not bow to stereotypes or be stopped by being told they're too short, too weak or too feminine, or they'll never learn.

They're skilled, proficient, determined. They have set their minds to accomplish something and then have done it. They are role models: interesting, fun-loving, full of moxie.

- **Independence.** Riding a motorcycle is a solitary pursuit. When we're riding, it's us and our motorcycle. Even when we're riding with a group, we're alone with our thoughts, our fears and our beliefs. When we ride, we alone make the decisions about how our motorcycle is ridden and where it goes. As we deal successfully with progressive challenges, the successes are ours to claim.

- **Community.** We all seek like-minded spirits, whether physical or spiritual, visible or invisible. Most new riders are amazed at the instant bond and the camaraderie and compassion among riders. Sometimes we've been searching for years for the right tribe to join. When we find our clan, though, we discover a common bond from which we not only derive strength as individuals, but also gather that strength to increase the cohesiveness of the community as a whole.

This change may begin within a group of motorcyclists, but the effects soon spread to other areas of our lives. This helps explain why motorcyclists tend to contribute extraordinary amounts of time and effort to charitable causes, nurturing the less fortunate and sharing with the community.

- **Balance.** Regardless of our DNA, we all carry feminine and masculine psychic characteristics, distinct from our biological gender. Both are essential to a vibrant life. Their dynamic tension must work together seamlessly in balance and harmony, or we lose power.

Historically in our culture, however, we have separated these two energies in men and women to the detriment of our authentic selves. Just as the masculine has been bred out of females, the

feminine has been bred out of males. So, we have the phenom-
enon of yin and yang. Yin, the female energy, is the receptor:
dark and in some ways passive. This is the energy we relate to
home, nurturing and community, and to being quiet and still.
It gives birth to our creativity. Yang, the male energy, is the
aggressor, outwardly focused and goal oriented. Its restlessness
calls to our desire for adventure. Yang is the spark that ignites
our creativity and brings our ideas into being. Both need to be
in balance in order to create a whole.

At first glance, a motorcycle is male psychic energy at its finest.
It thrusts us forward, it's forceful, directed, strong and dynamic,
and it satisfies our need for adventure. Without a rider, though,
without someone to channel its energy, it is powerless and goes
nowhere.

Riding fulfills a psychic need for women and gives their masculine energy an outlet. The motorcycle then becomes a receptor of
direction, instructions and the attributes of the feminine psyche.
The perfect psychic balance of feminine and masculine creates
the whole and is the power that moves us forward. Even the
relationship between rider and machine is a dynamic balance
between feminine and masculine energies.

In spite of the call to our wild nature, we resist going with it.
This happens with learning to ride or with many other challenges.
But almost any barrier can be overcome if one wants to learn to ride.
Ask Roxie Malone, who was told as a child she'd never walk, never
mind ride a motorcycle.

Resistance is caused by fear and causes us to do silly things, which
in turn drain our energy, make things much more difficult than they
need to be and prevent us from progressing. A woman I know was
so frightened by the stories she'd heard about motorcycles, she was
terrified to use the throttle. When she tried to move off, she'd release

the clutch, but she couldn't bring herself to activate the throttle. So, she would stall and lose her balance, which in turn reinforced her fear. I tried to get her to understand that using the power would make things much easier, but she never was able to get past the fear.

The potential sources of fear are many:

- **Cultural training.** Men originally wrote the rules for motorcycling and designed the game and the gear. Early women riders had to conquer this domination and defy societal expectations while riding bikes and wearing clothing designed for men. Even now, with greater participation of women, we're still in the minority and sometimes still need to buck the system.

- **Opinions of others.** Perhaps they'll think we're not feminine. Perhaps they'll think we're dykes. Families, friends and business associates all have an image of what a motorcyclist is. People regularly tell me, "But you don't look like a biker." But I *must* look like a biker, because I *am* one and have been for forty years. But what happens when someone who doesn't ride wants to ask you on a date? Or what if he does ride and his bike is smaller than yours? Before we can change the way others view us, we must change the way we view ourselves.

- **Safety concerns.** Families and friends worry about our safety, of course. Non-riders seem compelled to relate horror stories, complete with gruesome details of people who have been killed or maimed. But we know the risks and accept them and prepare for them. We overcome our fears and reap incredible rewards.

- **Dealing with change.** A ride is always an adventure to some degree. Things happen when we're out there. It starts to rain, there's gravel in a corner, someone cuts us off, a detour diverts our carefully planned route, our GPS stops working. The list is endless, and when we're motoring down the road on a five-hundred-pound-plus machine, things can unfold in a hurry.

We have to have our wits about us at all times. We learn to be prepared for the unexpected.

- **Physical requirements.** Am I strong enough to handle it? Am I capable of learning how to control it? What if I drop it? Potentially disabling thoughts abound, but motorcycling isn't about manhandling our bikes. When they're stopped, they're heavy and awkward to move around.

The smallest street bike starts at around two hundred and eighty pounds and most street bikes are at least four hundred and fifty pounds. When bikes are not under power, we're no physical match for their weight. Maintaining balance, particularly at slow speeds, is essential to staying upright. Learning to ride entails finding the bike that best suits your riding style, understanding how to control it and making it work for you.

- **Finding others to ride with.** If you don't know anyone you can ride with, it may take a bit of work and gutsiness, but other riders are out there to be found — probably looking for you. It has been my motorcycle that has led me to the most interesting people and places.

- **Fear of failure.** Admittedly, learning to ride can be daunting. If we fail to try, though, we have already failed. If we're not committed to learning to ride, we won't be successful.

- **Fear of success.** If I learn to ride a motorcycle, maybe I also have the skills to apply for that new job. If my image of myself changes, so do my expectations of myself and those of others around me. At the root of it all is the fear of what we will discover about ourselves through riding. Mastering the initial physical steps is only the beginning. We're alone when we ride and being alone with ourselves and our thoughts can make us feel very vulnerable. But once we've cracked the code to tapping into our capabilities and we discover the thrill of self-mastery, a whole new world opens up.

If we're going to get anywhere at all, we need to recognize whatever fear is holding us back, and leave it behind. Everyone I spoke with has her own method of doing this, some more effective than others. The bottom line is to address the irrationality, savor the present moment, park fear and move on.

Lois Pryce, who has traveled the world on solo adventures, thinks about the situation she's in — and she's been in some dandies — and asks herself whether she would rather be in this predicament, having an adventure and trying to sort it out, or back in her office cubicle. That always gets her through.

Our culture as a whole is going through a massive shift as it seeks a restoration of balance and new equilibrium. Women increasingly have careers in engineering, the military and skilled trades. Women choose to remain single longer, delay having children and end unfulfilling relationships. Men take a greater role in child rearing and household chores, and enter careers in elementary education and nursing. Most importantly, the notion of choice has become acceptable: men and women alike are being encouraged to choose what works best for them individually and for their families.

And more women are riding motorcycles.

Women riding out of their own choice are indicative of the evolution for men and women alike. Women are now freer to challenge and conquer something not traditionally thought of as a female pursuit. A man can be proud to share something important with his partner at his side.

I often see women and men begin motorcycle courses with fierce determination pushing through the looks of abject terror. Something inside them propels them forward, keeping them going until they succeed. And then you see a smile light up each face, and it doesn't go away.

This is the smile of the motorcycle rider. We have opened ourselves and connected with our souls. We're completely exposed to the elements with no protection and nothing to act as a barrier between us and nature. We're vulnerable, we're strong and we're free.

Women riders display a special energy, one others recognize and connect with. A bond is created by knowing we share the same freedoms and independence; by curiosity about what she had to go through to get here, who or what she had to challenge; and by a sense of relief that others are sharing the same experiences.

Many of the women I interviewed, however, don't even consider gender when they see another woman rider. Rather, they see a person who has talent, sets goals, makes plans and goes for it. And it's empowering to the observer to see someone else pushing through personal barriers, trying something new and testing limits.

Learning to ride is not so different from understanding ourselves. Once we understand what controls us, where our energy comes from, how we tap into it, what drains it, how to balance the myriad of choices and where it takes us, there's no stopping us.

Understanding our machines can play a big part in this. It's empowering to be able to diagnose and make at least basic repairs rather than giving that control to someone else. It can teach us as much about ourselves as we learn about the bikes. When we take our bike apart, we learn how it operates and discover that what we thought was so complex is really quite simple. It's all objective. There's no room for judgment, fears or biases. It's all logically sound. Similarly, we can break down complex challenges into their manageable components and what once seemed insurmountable becomes doable.

We also realize that everything is connected, including that we as people share a common spirit and source of power. If we allow ourselves to accentuate differences — gender, age, culture, values or even the type of motorcycle we ride — that separates us. Looking for what we have in common creates harmony and strengthens us all. We all have a role here on earth, and as we come to understand that we are connected to everything alive; we come to understand that everything that we do matters; we move to thoughts and behaviors with a positive effect on those around us.

Whether we're riding or facing a new challenge, we learn to look toward our destination, focus on our goal. We deal with the changes and bumps on the road, always maintaining control and momentum. Our mirrors tell us where we've been, and we check them often to learn from our past as we move ahead.

We have all had to use our strength to achieve what we've got, and women riders have had the extra hurdle of overcoming the maleness of motorcycling. We find a momentum reflected in many positive ways and can transfer that to many other areas of our lives.

CHAPTER 2

Perceptions on Power

"Riding taught me a lot about life and it's probably why I am such a success today. I can shut that thing off that says I can't do it."

—Star stuntwoman Debbie Evans Leavitt

I woke up at age forty-eight. I began to discover I had an untapped reservoir of power. Like flood water pushing against a levee, that reservoir was beginning to push against my self-erected barriers, opening the gate to the road that would bring me back to me.

The family, culture and society into which I arrived on this earth were instrumental in shaping the thoughts, attitudes and beliefs that guided my early behavior. Traditions, role models, religion, fairy tales and myths, all passed down from one generation to the next, set the expectations based on cultural norms, including expectations based on gender. A strong work ethic, kindness, compassion and core values were among the strengths. Conversely, there were many learned fears and an aversion to risk taking that had a great deal of influence on my confidence, self-esteem and perception of how much power I had.

The innate wild woman had been tamed, but as with anything else in nature, my sense of self was yearning to be free. It was only a matter of time until something would give so I could be authentic. The Bhagavad Gita avers that:

> "Even as a person casts off worn out clothes and puts on others that are new, so the embodied self casts off worn out bodies and enters into others that are new. This self cannot be cut, burnt, wetted or withered. Eternal, all-pervading, unchanging, immovable — the self is the same forever."

Understanding my own personal power, what it was, where it was, and the challenges that prevented me from using all of it, became a priority for me. I began to reflect on my life and how I had become trapped inside my shell. I needed to understand how I had gotten there so I could take back control, get back on track and stay there.

My relationship with riding and personal power has been inextricably intertwined throughout my life. My involvement with motorcycles has paralleled periods of growth in my life and taken me on an odyssey of self-discovery that carried me back to who I was.

My German ancestors embraced the Mennonite culture that emerged from Europe's Reformation in the Sixteenth Century. Known for their superior agricultural abilities, they caught the attention of Catherine the Great, who was seeking foreign settlers to colonize part of what is now the Ukraine. With promises of land and assurances they could keep their language, religion and traditions and live in self-contained colonies, they began migrating to this new country in 1789.[1]

---

[1] James Urry, *Mennonites, Politics and Peoplehood.* University of Manitoba Press, p. 85

The Mennonite tradition of which I speak is not the same as the "old order" horse and buggy Mennonites, or Amish. Ours was a more moderate version. People chose to live more in the world, although still separate from it.

My grandmother and her twin sister were born in 1898, and life was relatively good during their early years, but the Russian Revolution struck in 1917. Anarchy ruled. Parties of opposing soldiers, "Reds" and "Whites," in turn passed through villages, indiscriminately plundering and pillaging as they went, taking anything of value. Desperate robber gangs scavenged what was left.

My grandmother and the cousins she lived with erected a false wall in their barn to protect what little food and valuables they had: some grain, potatoes and beets — and a motorcycle. It was all they had, other than the personal strength and power of those who survived. The degree of hardship they experienced is unimaginable to me. Where they had once been prosperous farmers and peaceful, law-abiding citizens, they were now starving peasants, fearing for their lives at every moment. The government confiscated crops and seed grains, creating famine across the land.

My grandparents were able to flee in 1924, with barely more than the clothes on their backs. The motorcycle was left behind and, to my knowledge, my grandmother never rode a motorcycle after coming to Canada. Her sister, who is still living, did, though. When she was ninety-one, my eighty-year-old uncle took her for her first ride on his Honda Gold Wing.

My parents were born in Canada into the Mennonite Brethren culture and I was raised in that faith. I was blessed in that it was a culture of strong ethics, generosity and humanity, but it also discouraged questioning what you're taught. That made it difficult to believe in my personal ability to take charge of my life.

My arrival in this world was followed over the next twelve years by that of five siblings. How my parents managed to raise us all and survive financially on a fruit farm is still a mystery to me, for all the work ethic they passed on to us.

Out of necessity, gender was not much of an issue when it came to assigning work on the farm. We all learned to drive the tractor, pick cherries and harvest rhubarb by hand. Peaches were different. For some reason, the men and hired help picked the peaches, while the women stayed in the barn, sorting and packing the fruit for market.

When the time came for secondary school, I was bused to one run by the church. I was the Ugly Duckling. I didn't belong and I hated every moment there. I developed stomach ulcers. My restlessness with religious traditions had started and the first signs of rebellion were surfacing. After two years, I refused to go back and I moved to a public secondary school.

All the while I was growing up, I found the underlying values of love, charity, respecting and serving to be solid, and I embraced them then and still do. The fundamental "blind faith" part was a different matter.

"The end is near" was an ever-present threat to toe the line and I spent many years trying to be good. What if the rapture happened and I didn't make the cut because I was a doubter? Such fears hobbled me and insidiously usurped my power from an early age. I know now I don't need fabricated rules to tell me what's right and wrong, and my faith in God has never been stronger, but I had to move away from organized religion to appreciate and embrace this. It took forty-eight years and a few motorcycles to arrive at that awareness.

I was introduced to my first one when I was sixteen and my younger brothers paid eighty-five dollars for a used Honda 50 step-through to get around on our farm. My parents didn't bat an eyelash when that motorcycle came home. I was raised to be independent and to see me learn to ride never seemed like a big deal to them. To me, it was fun and a little adventure. I didn't even know about the barriers to riding until I heard others talking about them. The Honda was easy to learn on and it was just something we all did. A couple of years later, my brothers moved up to a 125cc Yamaha and that sealed my interest. From then on, a motorcycle was always there, waiting to take me to where I needed to go, physically or spiritually.

My early exposure to non-traditional thinking colored my perspective, and learning to ride didn't seem a big deal at the time. It was somewhat of a paradox. Conformity in a religion and culture were drilled into all of us, but something so non-traditional as a daughter riding a motorcycle was completely accepted.

Weather can make or break a farmer's season. I remember many times when everything looked so promising. Then a late frost would wipe out the peach blossoms. Or we had a bumper crop, but then I would see Dad standing at the open barn door on a hot, humid summer day, watching in helpless agony as hail beat down and in a few devastating minutes wiped out the entire harvest.

It wasn't until I was well into my motorcycle touring business that it dawned on me that I, too, had chosen a business heavily dependent on weather. Cold and rain deter clients. After all the weather disasters growing up, I had chosen something with the same hazards. That insight on the effect of our upbringing came to me as I was trying to understand my preoccupation with scarcity and financial hardship.

I followed my mother's footsteps into nursing, never imagining I was capable of going to university despite my outstanding grades. Besides, it intimidated me, and it wasn't done in our community. After I graduated from nursing and began working full time, I bought a 175 Honda XL and rode it back and forth to the hospital. I suppose it was unusual to some, but to me, it was just something I did.

I married a man who was kind, loving, intelligent, educated and resourceful, had a sense of humor, rode a motorcycle — and was from outside the "faith." I thought he could help get me away from it.

When I took a new name on my wedding day, I was shocked by my sense of loss and bewilderment. I attributed it to wedding-day jitters. I expected marriage to take me away to a whole new world. I didn't realize what a huge disservice I was doing to myself and my husband; nor did I have any inkling of how it would disperse my own power.

Our wedding gift to each other was a brand new motorcycle we could share, although the ownership was in my name. The symbolism escaped me at the time but that motorcycle was always there for me. I had given up my name but right there with me was my link to who I was.

Life was perfect. At least that's the way it appeared. I had a good husband, we both had well-paying jobs and promising careers, and the whole world awaited us.

But the cracks soon appeared. Within the first six months, I started having panic attacks and then became ill with mononucleosis. Attributing it all to rapid life changes, we carried on. It helped that we were close to beautiful countryside where we could escape and ride for hours.

My power was plastered over. My choices for both career and marriage partner were the outcome of my fear-based thinking and self-fabricated limitations. My inner guide was trying to talk but I was too afraid to listen. It drained my energy and left me ill.

I finally left hospital nursing in 1979 and migrated to occupational health nursing in a steel plant. Here was a spark of life as a fascinating new world opened up. It wasn't a usual field for a woman, but my years on the farm and my years of riding helped give me credibility and the ability to function effectively in a man's world.

Recession came, though, and the downsizing included me. By this time, my stomach ulcers were back. A few months later, an opportunity to operate a home nursing service presented itself and an entrepreneurial spirit I didn't know I had leapt at the chance. It was another sign of life.

I was no longer attending church, but I had been raised to believe marriage vows were sacred, so we were seeing a marriage counselor. Besides, it wasn't as though anything was overtly wrong. I kept reminding myself of all the good things in my life.

Motorcycling was calling to me, too. I found a lovingly used 750 BMW for my husband, so we each had our own bike. We enjoyed a lot of traveling. Now that I look back on it, regaining a motorcycle of my own signaled a grasp for strength and autonomy. Back at work, my career started heading toward corporate training.

Travel and exploring other ways of life seemed a way to liven things up a bit, so we began vacationing in foreign lands, often in third-world countries. It was eye-opening and provided clues about my own challenges. Fears run across all cultures; mine were not unique.

It was far from a quick process, though. I even became listless about motorcycling and we sold our bikes in the mid Nineties. It paralleled the apathy in my life at that time. Whatever personal power I was aware of had been buried beneath multiple layers of protection built to fend off the pain of an unsuccessful relationship, a life that held little meaning and a sense that I could do little about it.

We had good careers, earned good incomes, built a beautiful custom post-and-beam house in the country, traveled all over the world — and I was miserable. This couldn't go on forever. Eventually, that small inner voice that was crying through all those layers to be heard began to get some attention. The fates were conspiring to help me rediscover who I was and what I was here to do.

The stories in this chapter reflect how the environment in which we're raised can affect our perception of power and our personal capabilities. The education we receive during this time will do one of two things: it will nourish us and encourage us to be who we are with full knowledge and access our wild nature, or our nature will be covered over to varying degrees. When that happens, we will have to call on our warrior selves to find and release it again. These women reflect both perspectives — and what happens when we look at things differently.

Debbie Evans Leavitt

Occupation: stunt woman
Location: Hollywood, California
Age: 53
Riding Discipline: trials, off-road, street, stunts
Began Riding: 1964
Website: debbieevans.com, stuntrev.com

Debbie Evans is considered one of Hollywood's top stunt women. She began riding motorcycles at age six and competing at age nine. In 2003, she was inducted into the American Motorcyclist Association's Motorcycle Hall of Fame.

She has appeared as a motorcycle stunt rider and stunt performer in over three hundred movies and television programs. She has won seven Taurus World Stunt awards: for Best Work With a Vehicle in The Fast and the Furious *(2002) and* Date Night *(2011); Best Specialty Stunt in* Taxi *(2005); and Best Stunt by a Stuntwoman in* The Fast and the Furious, Matrix Reloaded *(2004),* Superman Returns *(2007) and* Wanted *(2008).*

Debbie was the first woman to ride well enough to compete against the men at the National and World Championship level in the Fédération Internationale de Motocyclisme's Trial World event. Finishing well ahead of any other women made her the unofficial women's champ.

As the only woman among two hundred and eighty entries at the Scottish International Six Days Enduro (ISDE), she finished fourth in the under 250 cc class and one hundred and ninth overall, effectively silencing the British men who were betting on which day she would DNF (Did Not Finish).

Debbie has road-raced at Daytona and won many trophies for desert enduros. She has been married for thirty-two years and raised three children, proving that women can balance career and family.

I've never let other people's perceptions of what I should be able to do stop me from doing anything. If I had, I would never have accomplished anything. A prime example of this was when I was asked to do some road-bike stunt work for the movie *Torque*. I have an extensive motorcycle-riding background, but they were asking me to do things I'd never done. If I had gone out and polled a hundred people on, "Do you think a mother of three in her mid-forties could learn these tricks?" what do you think they would have said?

Probably because of my motorcycling background, the thought never even crossed my mind until later. On the first day, I was doing seat stands, tank stands, rolling burnouts[2], and crossovers[3]. On the second day, I was skitching[4] off the back and side, doing crossover wheelies and endos[5]. Riding taught me a lot about life. It's probably why I am such a success today, because I can shut off that thing that says, "No, you can't do it." Or, "It hurts too much. Stop!" You'll never get to the finish that way.

My first motorcycle at age nine came from a junkyard. It was a box of parts, all spray-painted blue, even the wheels. Wearing a hood to protect my eyes, I stood at the wire wheel, meticulously cleaning every part. Then my dad and I put it all together. I had my first bike — and schooling in mechanics and patience.

As a kid, I didn't fit in much because I was a tomboy. I got a lot of ridicule. I loved anything active and outside, and because few other girls were riding I competed against the boys. When I got out on my motorcycle on the weekends, I thought, "Who cares? You guys are all

---

[2] While rolling forward, apply the front brake and rev the engine at the same time. Pop the clutch, causing the rear tire to spin. Can be done in a straight line, zigzags or a circle. Makes very nice smoke!

[3] Sit on the tank with your legs over the front of the motorcycle.

[4] Get the bike going about 45 mph, click it into neutral, and slide yourself off the back so that your feet are dragging behind it. I connect a strap across the seat so I have something to brace myself on and then, when I'm ready to get back on, I just put more pressure on my feet, it pops me up and I pull the bike underneath me.

[5] Grab your front brake, making the rear wheel come up.

a bunch of losers." In fifth grade, I was already riding with the wind in my face and all that junk was falling off behind me. Eventually, everybody has some difficult part in their life. Nobody gets away unscathed. Motorcycles are very healing when it comes to that.

I always liked Trials because of the challenge. I enjoyed competing against myself as much as someone else. I could go off, find a challenging rock and just keep going at it until I made it over the first time. Then I'd have a couple of bad times where I didn't do well, but I'd keep going until I mastered it.

Early on, I had other lessons in perseverance. At age eleven, my parents and I were competing in a little Poker Run Enduro in the desert. I was miffed when my mom fell and I figured I'd go on ahead on my own. Rain turned to snow, which obscured the markings. Somehow I got off course and I decided to wait on a hill where I had a better perspective. Many people were lost and I could see them wandering around in the desert.

Freezing, hungry, alone and finally crying, I waited and waited for a familiar face. At long last, a friend of my dad found me and we made our way back. You don't know you can go through something like that until you do. Too many people give up before they reach victory or even get close to being a success, because they tell themselves it can't be done. To keep going even when it's rough, when I was so tired, everything hurt and I wanted to stop, is tough. But I knew that if I kept going I would get to the finish.

Stunts have taught me how to calculate and manage risk. When I first got the call to work on the movie *Deathsport* with David Carradine and Claudia Jennings, they wanted me to jump a thirty-foot ravine on an old Yamaha DT 400, clad with about seventy pounds of metal to make it look futuristic. I had never jumped that far on a motorcycle with nothing underneath me. We set up a ramp, measured out the distance on a road, made the jump and measured how far we'd gone. We kept progressively increasing the jump until we were at the distance plus five and doing it every single time. I had no speedometer, so I had to be dialed in to the sound of the motor. I knew what I needed to do and got it done because I focused on the landing.

If you don't have a healthy sense of fear, you're going to get hurt. In stunting, we take calculated risks, look at everything, dissect it, plan it to make it as safe as possible. We want to go to work the next day. It's very much like riding Trials. You walk each section and figure out the best line through.

When you get on a movie set, everything becomes very confined. There are cameras, C-stands, people, cars coming in from here and there and all these obstacles that you need to deal with down to the smallest detail. The skills I need here all come from what I've learned from motorcycling. You don't want to look at the thing that you don't want to hit, because your body will go there. So you look where you want to go.

Even so, at age forty-nine, I had a very bad accident on *Yes Man*. I was riding a motor scooter with Jim Carrey's double on the back. We'd done the shot a whole bunch of times, but this time one of the cars was off on its speed, causing another car to hit me. I had multiple fractures, got knocked out and was hospitalized for nineteen days.

I've learned through motorcycle riding not to look at the problem but to look at the goal. So, I'm back to work. Many people wouldn't even think that they could get back to work — or even try. That thought never even crossed my mind. It was just a matter of when. In less than a year, I was back on my motorcycle. My trust in God helped. I think I can remember maybe two days when I was thinking, "Why me?"

My mechanical background has given me a great deal of confidence in all areas of my life. I know that many women are afraid to do something because of what may happen. If they can learn basic mechanics so they have an understanding of the motorcycle and start with short trips, whether it's on the road or dirt, the difference is amazing. Learning mechanics and learning to ride correctly is very freeing. It gives you a sense of power and a sense of peace. It helps you to overcome that fear of the unknown.

I was a girl. I wasn't supposed to play sports. I wasn't supposed to ride motorcycles. When I got into the business I was told, "You can't be married and be a stunt woman. It just doesn't work. None of the marriages work." My husband and I have been married for thirty-two years. Or, "If you have kids, you can kiss your career goodbye." Well, I have three kids.

It's a lifestyle and you can make choices. When the kids got old enough, they'd ride on the back. Steve rode his own bike with no training wheels at age four, Daniel at three and Rebecca at five. We used to go camping and riding together on dirt bikes. It's a great family sport. We took the kids all the way to Tennessee and they competed in the youth nationals. My daughter finished first in her class and my son Daniel's got two national championships for his age group.

It's funny, because when I had the last two kids, I thought, "Maybe I shouldn't be doing this," and I backed off for a bit. I wasn't as happy. Somebody talked me into going back to work because they really needed me. I went and came home happy and energized. I realized that God gave me these gifts and talents and I'm better to everyone, including myself, if I'm using those gifts. Everybody's got a gift that they've been given and something they enjoy doing and they should be able to express themselves in that way.

When I was talking to my dad the other night, it was just so clear that I'm a confident, independent person because of my motorcycling. I love my family and want to have them around me. It's not that kind of independence. It's just that I can take off and go anywhere and feel completely fine. I like to tell other people, and especially women, "Don't let other people's opinions stop you. If you've got a dream in your heart, figure out a way to make it happen. You can do it!"

Lise Grenier

Occupation: provincial motorcycle coordinator, Ontario Provincial Police president, Ontario Association of Police Motorcycle Instructors; ride master, OPP Golden Helmets Motorcycle Precision Riding Team
Location: Orillia, Ontario
Age: 43
Riding Discipline: street
Began Riding: 1992

Lise is becoming legendary as she has progressed steadily through the ranks of the motorcycling division of the Ontario Provincial Police.

Twenty-one years ago, when she started her career, you would have been hard pressed to find two more solidly male bastions than the police force and motorcycling. Lise never considered she couldn't do either. She was raised with traditional values and believed she could do anything she set her mind to.

She can ride circles around just about anyone on her big police Harley, and she is an extraordinary leader and mentor to an ever-widening circle of protégées.

I joined the OPP (Ontario Provincial Police) Force in 1988 and was posted at the Port Credit Detachment near Toronto — totally out of my element. I was the youngest of eight, born and raised on a farm near Sturgeon Falls, a small town in northern Ontario, so it was a bit of a culture shock. I had to mature fairly quickly and develop confidence to deal with whatever came up.

In 1992, the OPP offered a three-week motorcycle course. That sounded pretty cool. On your first day, you had to pick up this eight hundred and fifty pound Harley-Davidson Police Special, and thank God they taught some techniques for that. We took those motorcycles through every road surface possible, grass, sand, asphalt and bushes: everywhere that could come up during enforcement.

By the time I graduated, I was bruised in every way possible, but I loved it. If it's raining or if it's snowing, you don't want to be out there in some ways, but I still say the worst day on a motorcycle is better than the best day in a car.

The course itself boosted my confidence because it was all male instructors and I was the only woman student. Deep inside I was thinking, "I'm going to show them I can do this job." In 1988, some men didn't think it was a job for women. Now it's different. Getting out there and working in what I was trained to do made a big difference in thinking with both the male officers and me.

In 1997 I joined the OPP Golden Helmets Precision Riding Team and in 1999 I became an instructor. I actually came and taught all these people in the OPP how to ride! I had to show them first that I'm capable of doing this stuff and I can actually teach them how to do that. In a lot of cases, I'd have to get on the bike and start whipping through some cones and doing some tight turns just to prove it.

Later, I became heavily involved in the Ontario Association of Police Motorcycle Instructors and am now the president. We introduced the Great Lakes Police Training, four days every year for police officers on motorcycles from across Canada and the United States to improve their riding skills. We include a bit of a rodeo, ending with a friendly competition. I'm pretty pleased that this year I came in fourth out of one hundred and twenty riders.

Last year I was promoted into a new position, Provincial Motorcycle Coordinator. I'm responsible for ensuring all the motorcycles have been properly equipped so the officers can do their jobs.

I'm the Ride Master for the twenty people on the Golden Helmets. I'll tell you they're the best bunch of guys to work with. The fact that I'm a woman just doesn't faze them whatsoever. I'm also in charge of the VIP escorts for any dignitaries coming into town: the Prime Minister and any Presidents. I've escorted the Pope, the Queen, Lady

Diana and Prince Charles in 1991. I actually cared for the two boys, Prince William and Prince Harry, for ten days, doing things like taking them to McDonald's or swimming.

We deal with a lot with children, especially with the Golden Helmets performances. The kids can approach us and talk to us. We travel the province, sell regalia during our performances and donate the proceeds to a children's charity.

After a performance, the women and girls all line up at the "girl's" bike to meet me and congratulate me. I get that a lot and it's a really good feeling. I get silly comments, too, mostly from men, about special concessions because I am a woman, so it pleases me to tell them, guess what, I trained all these guys here.

Riding my own personal bike, a 1996 Electra Glide, is a completely different experience. When you're on a police bike, people are staring at you and not paying attention to the road and you have to be careful. You're scanning around you all the time — which you should do all the time anyway — but you're also looking for violations or you're looking for whatever call you're going to. But on your own bike, it's awesome. You get on it and you don't know where you're going and you go wherever you want.

It's awesome to see other women riders. I think there was a time when there weren't many women riding, but there really isn't anything you can't do, as long as you put your head, your heart and your passion into it. Then you can do anything.

Toni Sharpless

Occupation: district sales manager for a Canadian Powersports distributor
Location: Newmarket, Ontario
Age: 48
Riding Discipline: street
Began Riding: 1965: ice racing at 10; flat tracking at 16; road racing at 22; motocross at 31; hockey at 41

Toni is a silent hero. She grew up in a motorcycling family, yet I daresay the first time you meet her, "biker" would not come to mind. I saw her again at the motorcycle show last year. She's tall, beautiful and poised, with a wonderful sense of humor. I expect most of the people she was interacting with that day had no idea of her tremendous racing skills, the history she created and the road she has paved for others.

Toni purposefully pursued a racing career and was competing internationally in Japan and Europe before the concept of "women and motorcycling" became popular.

She says racing helped her to learn nothing comes easy, but if you set goals and work at it, you can be successful. Her skills helped her defeat cancer.

To Toni, talent is talent whether it comes in a man or a woman. And she's got plenty of it — whether it's racing motorcycles on the road or ice or through the forest, playing hockey or just being herself.

In November, Toni is being inducted into the Canadian Motorcycle Hall of Fame, joining her brother Blair.

Two younger brothers and I are all separated in ages by one and a half years. The Christmas when I was six years old, we woke up and found a mini bike under the Christmas tree. Just one. So we learned how to share and to ride motorcycles.

My mom didn't ride. She rode our mini bike once and ended up face first in an ant hill. We ran over to rescue the bike, not her. My father was a competitor in the Fifties and Sixties primarily. Dad would compete and we would ride around in the pits while he was racing. As my father got arthritis, he rode a street bike to and from work but he couldn't compete anymore. Maybe once a year he'd go out to one of our events, but he got involved in playing bridge, which became his passion. I remember my grandfather saying it wasn't fun to play golf anymore because he couldn't hit the ball as far as he got older. So I could understand why my dad wouldn't want to go and watch racing when he couldn't do it anymore.

I went to Mosport Raceway in Ontario to see a road race in 1982. I was standing next to the track on the infield, and once the bikes went by at full speed, I went, "Wow, I've got to try this." And that was it. I bought an RD 350LC Yamaha motorcycle, stayed up all night prepping it, loaded it into my van early in the morning and went off to race in Michigan. You had to wear a big orange safety vest with a big X on your back to identify you to all the other racers as a beginner and you might do something stupid out there. I wore the big neon bull's-eye on my back, took off from the back of the pack and ended up fifth in my first race. The challenge, the risk and speed hooked me. I raced that weekend, the whole rest of the summer and for the next ten years.

I didn't meet another woman racer in the United States or Canada until I met Kathleen Coburn later on in 1982 at Shannonville. She was the only other woman on the circuit. I was working on my bike and she came over to say hello. That's how our friendship started, and we're still friends.

I had actually done ice racing with my brothers when I was nine years old, and no women were ice racing either. Then we went into dirt track and no women were in dirt tracking either. I was very comfortable with it and didn't know any better.

All I wanted to do was race, and at times I was just about living out of my van. I got rid of my apartment and moved in with my aunt, who had a garage, which was quite appealing. My uncle had died and my mom was afraid my aunt was getting lonely, so Mom put a nomad together with a lonely person with a garage. I lived with my aunt for about four years of road racing and it was great.

The biggest thing to overcome was trying to get enough money to do it. I was paid very well for a young person back then, so I could afford the racing. The only problem was that practice was always on Fridays and I couldn't make it. I would show up Saturday morning and have to jump right into the qualifying races. With sponsors, I tried to really give them their money's worth, but I still felt like I was out there having fun doing what I really wanted to be doing and getting my sponsors to pay for it.

The biggest sponsor I had was Yamaha. In 1987, I was racing in Daytona on a Yamaha FZR 750 Superbike and made it to the front row of the second grid. It was the first time a woman had made it to the actual race. My bike had blown up on me in practice so I was scrambling around the pits trying to find parts and went over to the Yamaha pits. Some Japanese men were there with Yamaha shirts, wearing Yamaha running shoes and Yamaha shorts. And I thought, wow, these guys must be high up at Yamaha. So I went over to them and explained my problem but they didn't understand English very well. After I got my bike back together, qualified and made it to the grid, they came over to my pit, introduced themselves and congratulated me.

On the way home, I stopped at my mom's place near Windsor, Ontario, and she said some Japanese guys had called, left a Japanese phone number and wanted me to call them. When I got through, they told me they wanted me to come and race in the biggest race they have there, the Suzuka eight-hour endurance series. I was out of my skin. They said they'd pay for everything and build me a really fast bike. They asked me who I would want as my racing partner. I picked Kathleen Coburn, who had also done well at Daytona but had been on a Suzuki, so they didn't see her. "Two women? This is even better."

The next thing we know we're on a plane going over to Japan. We got off the plane and all these cameras were clicking and aiming toward us. We were looking over our shoulders figuring Brooke Shields was on the plane, so all of the shots they have is us looking over our shoulders. They took our bags, carried all of our gear and they gave us each a bouquet of flowers. It was a whirlwind with press conferences, practicing and racing on the private Yamaha track with awesome equipment. It was such a thrill. We ended up racing in the Suzuka eight-hour endurance race for two years. In 1987 through 1989, we also raced in the LeMans twenty-four-hour and Bola D'or twenty-four-hour races in Europe. Every time we came back to Canada, our heads would deflate and our feet would get firmly planted on the ground again because we'd get off the flight and nobody would be there. We'd be sitting on top of our pile of equipment waiting for a taxi.

I always said to myself when I was racing that I was going to race in world championships. I raced in Daytona but I wanted to race in a world championship outside of North America, and that was my next goal. I just kept saying that out loud and kept racing, trying to get better equipment and faster, and then it finally happened. There were a lot of ups and downs. If you get hurt, you have to take time out to heal, and then everybody else is getting faster while you're just sitting around healing.

My brother and I ran a trail-riding school for a few years. In our third year of operation, a woman phoned us up and said she really wanted to come out to the school and learn how to ride a dirt bike. She'd never ridden one and she had only one hand. We initially turned her down, but she was persistent.

Finally my brother came up with an idea to modify the bike so she could operate everything on one side of the handlebars, and we decided to give it a go. She came out and he taught her how to ride, and man she did really well. You know, it wouldn't have mattered if it was a woman or a guy with one hand. I was impressed. She made up her mind to do something, worked at it and didn't let anything get in her way.

My motorcycle experiences and accomplishments taught me to overcome things you think are impossible by persevering and stubbornness. I think I had some of those traits before I went racing, but they've become stronger and I've learned how best to use them. I've learned how to overcome things. In 1991, I got diagnosed with cancer, so I had to use all that positive stubbornness to get through that. Racing really helped me learn the lessons of life in that nothing comes easy and you've got to work for it.

I'm not expecting people to look at me and be impressed because I'm a woman, so I don't really see that in other people. What impresses me is really good talent. Like a guy who wins a championship, that kind of talent, that kind of level. Then I'm impressed.

Madeleine Marques

Occupation: paralegal, motorcycle training instructor
Location: Oakville, Ontario
Age: 43
Riding Discipline: street
Began Riding: 1992

Madeleine had to battle against her family's and then her husband's belief that women were subservient. She almost lost herself through low self-esteem and low self-confidence. Learning to ride helped in the fight.

I remember like it was yesterday a time when I was maybe eleven or twelve and my mom and dad and I were on our way home from our annual Florida vacation. It was cold and pouring rain. Dad pulled into a gas station, and he and my mom ran into the convenience store.

My dad did things totally on the cheap. We slept in the car in the middle of the night in some truck stop. I'd been in that car for two days and was ready to be tied up. I was alone, sitting on my knees, staring out the back window, thinking, "God help me," and I heard this rumble in the distance that sounded like thunder. It was getting closer and closer, and then some riders emerged from the gloom.

Wow, a pack of bikers. And the first one, the leader of the pack, was a woman! She pulled into the pump closest to my dad's car and nothing existed at that moment other than her. I didn't know the difference between bikes but I remember thinking hers was huge and she's so tiny and she's completely soaked. She was wearing a black leather jacket, black leather pants and an open face helmet and she had a wet, big, thick, long blonde braid down her back. She put her kickstand down, got off and came up to the pump and everything looked completely natural and easy. She filled up her bike, paid, looked around, gave a little hand signal to everybody, they all started up and off they went. I was in awe of the coolest woman on the entire planet.

I wondered what it was like to be her. Ever since then, I had this little thought in the back of my mind that maybe someday I could learn to ride a motorcycle, although I could never be as cool as her.

I never explored it any further and then I got married and we moved up to the country, where we were very isolated. My husband's hobby as a musician took him away most evenings, and during the day, he was at his full-time job, so I hardly ever saw him. I was desperately unhappy and took all kinds of night courses to fill the time. One evening, as I flipped through the college calendar to select the next course, my focus shifted as a group of bikes rode past. It was like when I was transfixed from the back seat of the car. I was living in a gray blur and the motorcycles had caught my attention. Coincidentally, the course calendar was open to the basic rider training course. It had to be a sign.

I decided to try it, much to the dismay of my husband: "Not another of your crazy ideas. Go ahead, take the course, but don't expect me to support you on it."

At the time I was a meek, quiet little thing without a lot of self-confidence and with an aversion to challenging myself. I didn't really expect to get my license. I came home that day, got out of the car and even though I was exhausted from the course, had this burst of energy and felt like I could have skipped and hopped and jumped all the way down the driveway. The next day, I began searching for a used bike. His exact words were, "Over my dead body." I gave it up but I grew increasingly resentful and bitter.

We ended up in marriage counseling. The big issue for me was he wouldn't *let* me ride a motorcycle. The counselor, to whom I am eternally grateful, persuaded my husband to *let* me ride. My husband came out bike shopping with me and we bought the first bike I saw, a little 450.

On my first ride, my low self- confidence screamed at each stop sign, but I had to continue because all I could do was straight-line riding. Finally, dusk made me get off. With all of my one hundred and three pounds, sweating and straining, I wrestled the bike back and forth until it was pointing in the opposite direction, back toward home.

Overcoming my own feelings of not being strong enough was one of my greatest challenges. Changing that went against every family grain, every marital grain. Besides, I didn't know a soul who rode. Interestingly, when my husband saw how much I was enjoying it, he took it out one evening and decided he wanted one, too. I was happy to have a partner to ride with, but he was still so busy we managed it only on the occasional Sunday afternoon.

Eventually the marriage ended. My motorcycling world instantly opened up. Within the month motorcycles were pulling into my driveway as I met riders I could be friends with. I feel sorry for that poor little girl who took so long to start riding, and I barely recognize her now.

The motorcycle was what awakened my power. It's not for every-body, and either you're meant to do it or you're not. But if it's for you, it's part of your soul. I was born with power, and riding was the catalyst that brought it out. Motorcycling is who I am. I teach it, I talk to people about it. My closest, most meaningful friends all ride. It's in every fiber of what I do. Everything in my living room is about motorcycles. It has changed who I am. If it's born in you, you don't even have to look for it. It comes and helps you be who you are. It helps you be stronger, more powerful and more masculine. You learn how to do some of your own wrenching and change your oil and stuff, and that's a really good feeling. It helps you be more feminine, too, through challenging your femininity. You're always putting on dark, heavy leather jackets and big chunky boots, so you've got to keep lipstick on.

The tentacles of how motorcycling has made a difference run everywhere, primarily because it has built confidence and that affects everything. Once you prove to yourself you can do it, you think, "Wow, I did that? Maybe I could do something else." For example, I used to be terrified of public speaking and now I speak easily in front of fifty students. If I overcame the forces from family, my husband and a monstrous motorcycle that seemed overpowering to me, I can overcome anything.

The best motorcycle experience can happen on any road and you know at that moment God is speaking directly to you. It may be a smooth, twisty road flanked by a peacefully flowing river and a rock face surrounded by forest; or a beautiful, warm, sunny day with no one around. All of the elements of heaven and earth are there. There's nothing better than this. I can do anything!

Juanita Losch-Finlan

Occupation: mother, server at upscale restaurant
Location: Toronto, Ontario
Age: 35
Riding Discipline: street, sidecar
Began Riding: 2009

Mark Richardson, editor of the Wheels Section of the Toronto Star, author of Zen *and* Now *and an avid rider, works with Juanita's husband and was familiar with Juanita, the boys and the family's exploits. Knowing the subject of this book, Mark suggested I speak with her.*

As soon as I arrived, the boys had to gear up with helmet and goggles and show me how they ride in Sidecar Sally. Juanita and I chatted on the back deck of her downtown Toronto home with her eldest son, who at five is already riding a dirt bike, sitting on her lap part of the time.

This remarkable woman began riding when her sons were eighteen months and three years of age. She has been able to balance the unique challenges that accompany combining the desire to ride with raising young children. The sidecar has become their summer vehicle and they've become celebrities, with frequent requests to have their photos taken. She is instilling lessons in her children at an early age about adventure, addressing fear and knowing you can do whatever you want, regardless of what others think.

I have always been adventuresome. I was backpacking in England and Scotland when I was sixteen. In my mid-twenties, I backpacked for a year, stopping in Northern India for a stint to teach English to monks and live in the monastery.

I married a motorcycle enthusiast and was quite comfortable riding pillion. When our first son was a baby, we started saving for a sidecar. By the time our second son had arrived, I thought, if I don't get on it, I'm going to be left alone. When the kids are older, they're going to be off with their dad doing everything and I'm going to be sitting at home doing nothing. I decided to try to get my license. I loved it right away. At the first break I called my husband and told him I was going to have my own bike!

The bike is now our summer vehicle. I use it to commute to work and I take the boys all over the city with it. Because I have the kids, I don't have the opportunity to get out and go on a ride with other adults when I'm in the city. My schedule and itinerary are so different. It's not about me. It's about them being impatient in the sidecar or how long, how far, how hot, who's fighting, who's not, who's lost his tutu, who's lost his blankee.

It's really neat to incorporate doing something together with my family into motorcycling. It's fun, we all enjoy it and it opens up so many more options. I'd rather be with them than riding by myself. When you have a family, you're on a budget, everyone has their own thing. But for us a family day is to get up, have our breakfast, pack a picnic lunch, gear up and head out on the road, maybe taking all day to go to the country and having an ice cream and a coffee. Then we stop at a park to go swimming along the way back. We always incorporate something for the children so it's fun for them, too.

I'm watching all the time. If anything happened, I'd feel terrible, so I stay in tune with what's happening with them, all around us, making sure they're one hundred and ten percent safe from *anything*.

We always made it a point that, even if we were just going to the corner store and back, you had to wear your gloves, boots and your helmet or you're not going. Safety is always first and we wanted to engrain that into the boys. We've developed a communication system: they will tug on my leg if they need something, there are hand signals to use if we have to pull over, we have the A-OK and the thumbs up. Eventually they're probably going to ride motorcycles, or get involved in some other adventures, and it's good they have that general know-how right from the beginning.

Our cottage vacation last summer was my most memorable riding experience to date. It was a learning time for me and a wonderful family adventure all rolled into one. I was learning to ride, learning the challenge of the motorcycle, paying attention and looking down the road. Focusing. That part of it was just really something for ME.

We packed our sleeping bags in rainproof sacks and bungeed them onto the back along with our rain gear; our clothing was in the side cases and we tucked a cooler into the toe of the side car so the kids could get a juice box if they needed it. Everything was color coded so we could keep straight what belonged to who. It's a lot of work when you have a family. It's not just ten minutes like you would take for yourself. It takes a good hour to get going, but it's also a lot of fun.

My husband rode the brunt of the heavier highways and as soon as we got onto the back roads, he pulled over and sat on the back. The person on the back always has to be on the watch — making sure the gear was attached, making sure the kids were safe, they weren't fighting — and let the motorist focus on riding. When we got up toward the cottage, there was more opportunity for me to drive because there wasn't that much traffic and the roads were long and winding.

I cut my teeth on those roads. He would take the kids and I'd go out myself for an hour or so. I learned something new each and every time I went out — about the level of the road or how the sidecar was sitting or how I could improve my turns by using the back brake. It gave me something for ME and kept me stimulated. It was very relaxing, too. I would come home feeling charged.

My most challenging experience was this spring when we decided to go up to my parents' farm. Strong winds surprised us on the way, accompanied by rain and hail. It was just wild but I felt good afterward. It gave me a sense of new heights as a motorcyclist. If I can do this, I can do anything safely.

It was a lesson for the boys as well. We weren't afraid. We stopped several times under a bridge and lifted the top on the sidecar to check on the boys. "Yeah, we're good Mom, we're good." Once we arrived, they were like, "Wow, Mom, you did GREAT!"

I am instilling a sense of adventure in my boys. They don't watch a lot of TV or go to traditional amusement parks, yet they have just as much fun. We all go out on the motorcycle, stop somewhere for lunch where there's a great big dirt pile and they climb all over it. That's the highlight of their day. It's imaginative, it's creative, it gives them a sense of not being afraid of new challenges, new things — if they want to do it, they can do it.

Nancy Irwin

Occupation: writer, journalist, activist, gardener
Location: Toronto, Ontario
Age: 48
Riding Discipline: street, dual-sport, off-road
Began Riding: 1979

Nancy Irwin came to my rescue the day I crashed in the woods. I had read her columns in a national motorcycle magazine for years but met her in person for the first time when we both signed up for the off-road training program.

Nancy questioned societal rules around traditional roles right from the start. It made no sense to her that boys could ride motorcycles and girls couldn't. Coming from very different backgrounds, we were both intrigued by each other's stories.

She stands up for what she believes in, lives life to the fullest and isn't afraid to go against the grain. She's been successful because from a young age, she was encouraged to question the status quo, even when it was politically incorrect. That characteristic has enabled her to seize opportunities and meet people and be part of a larger contribution to her community. It was also an excellent example of how early education influences how our life rolls out.

I met a Vespa when I was five or six and the boy up the street would graciously take us kids on rides of half a block every now and then. He might have done it only a handful of times but, believe me, I absolutely cherished it. Growing up, my bicycle was my transportation and my freedom. I really loved the feeling of riding it and would ride for hours. I still do. One day, I realized there were motorcycles and they were within my reach and could take me farther faster, but the basic feeling was the same. Moving to a motorcycle was a natural progression. By the time I was twenty, I had learned to ride and purchased my own motorcycle.

I'm sure riding a motorcycle wasn't the first thing I did that I wasn't supposed to do. Almost everything that happened was because I was a girl and they said I couldn't do this or I couldn't do that. Even from an early age, I didn't buy that for a moment. It made absolutely no sense then and still doesn't.

Riding a motorcycle sets you apart. You cannot walk into an office or have an office job and look like everyone else if you ride a motorcycle. You arrive in a great big coat, great big pants, great big boots, and you look like a blimp.

I did not feel adequate riding a motorcycle without learning how to fix it. When things would break down, I was in a position to deal with it. I wasn't helpless. Later, I enrolled in a college aircraft mechanics course for six months full time and apprenticed with two mechanics. That, too, put me in a position of power because it was not only meaningless for men to be telling me I wouldn't be riding a motorcycle, but most of them didn't know what I know about mechanics.

The college had primarily trades programs, so the students and faculty were predominantly male. I was the only woman in my class of twenty-five. There was a secretarial program and it was filled with women. Sexual harassment was horrendous and the teachers did nothing to stop it. The dean moved the secretarial school to the front of the building, right across from his office, so the women wouldn't have to walk through the hallways. They were also let out half an hour earlier to minimize the chances of interaction with the guys. That left me in the back with all the guys.

One day a man come up to me in the hallway and said, "Come with me." I thought, "This is it. This is just it." But I went with him — and he introduced me to somebody who was so thrilled to meet me, someone who had a sister who wanted to ride. That turned out to be a really positive experience. But the fear of harassment and physical harm had become so great I was in tears every day on the way to school, and I thought I'd learned enough by then. That was my last day there.

In 1987, I left Toronto for what I thought was going to be a two-year trip around the world. Five years later, I came back briefly and then went out west. In Belize I met someone I ended up traveling with through the rest of Central and some of South America. Then I met someone in Boston and we went off to Europe, and later to Africa and Asia.

I've learned things like drywall, plaster, electrical, plumbing, pipefitting, carpentry, roofing and body work, but motorcycles are the non-traditional things I really started with. They're so publicly visible, and once you bust through that barrier, other barriers are easier to break. It's also a lot less radical now than it was thirty years ago, but I think I underestimated the long-term effects at the time.

My present would have been so different without motorcycles that it's kind of incomprehensible. When I bought my first house, my father said, if I ever got in any kind of trouble financially, I could always sell my motorcycle to help pay for the house. I said, "Are you kidding? I'd sell the house before I'd sell the motorcycle."

Holly Ralph

Occupation: retired elementary school teacher
Location: Ancaster, Ontario
Age: 64
Riding Discipline: street
Began Riding: 1991

Now in her sixties, Holly didn't buy into what she was taught about roles and expectations. She defies all stereotypes of women riders.

I'm five feet two inches if I really stretch, very small-boned and sixty-five years old, so I'm not what you would think of as a biker babe. I have osteoporosis and I'm not really supposed to be riding bikes, but until I break something, I'm going to ride. Motorcycling is very empowering, especially when you're perceived as a little old lady who should be riding one of those old folks' scooters.

My first boyfriend had a motorcycle and I loved riding on the back for years. Finally, at age forty-seven, after the kids were out of the way, I got my license and started riding on my own.

I was the chief timer and scorer at races for about ten years so I was very involved in racing. When they did the Vintage Christie Sprints at the Christie conservation area here, I couldn't resist. I took my Bridgestone and raced up the hills. At the end, I grabbed the brakes on a left-hand turn and high-sided right in front of a world champion who was watching. He was the perfect gentleman. When I met him, of course I was unconscious for quite a while but he saw to it I was looked after. I came to and went to the banquet and he was just so lovely.

My toughest motorcycle moment was riding a steep, twisty downhill on the Grand Piton in heavy, loose gravel. I started downhill and went to shift into a lower gear and hit neutral and just took off, way too fast. It was just turn after turn after turn in loose gravel, and I don't like off-road riding to begin with. It was so steep and I was in the middle of this one-lane road thinking, if anything's coming up, I'm going to hit them going around the curve. I didn't dare touch the clutch or the brakes. Finally, I got to where I thought it was flattening out a little bit and tried touching the levers and took off over the berm. I hit a rotten log, which exploded and dumped me over, and I landed under the bike. Somebody following me got the bike off me. I rode back and put ice onto my head, my leg and everywhere else I had bumps and bruises. The next day, I found a place that replaced the wind screen and banged a few things back into position on the bike. I avoid loose gravel now.

You have to get right back on or your fears will take control. Even after the Christie sprints, which resulted in a really bad concussion and damaged arm, as soon as I could ride again, I went and rode back up that hill just to do it. If the trauma is greater than the pleasure you get out of riding, I could see you wouldn't get back on. For me there's enough pleasure I want to get back on.

I've learned also to listen to my intuition more. One of my bikes is an old BMW and an ad describes them as being unstoppable. Mine was, and people kept saying the bike didn't have a problem, "It's just that you've got such little tiny hands and the brakes are heavy." I kept saying, "I don't think so." When I finally took it in, the mechanic said, "You know, you've got absolutely no brakes." I said, "I've been trying to tell people that for ages." It's amazing how much more fun it is to ride a bike when it actually has brakes.

Riding alone is my favorite way to go and every year I ride my 250 Yamaha Virago to Colorado. Going out and riding long distances, and not booking ahead because I don't know what the day will bring and I want to enjoy the experience, is such a confidence builder. I just leave when I want in the morning, stop when I feel like it, and it's really great being out there on my own, doing what I want when I want.

Last year I bought a spot tracker so my kids could see where I am all the time and I wouldn't have to call and reassure them. They all wrote back and said, "That's a lot of money. Why bother?" They're so used to me being off all summer long riding that it hadn't occurred to them that maybe they should be worried about me.

I've always seen women riding and women racing and women involved. And the one thing I don't want to see is women separated out and being coddled.

There is nothing like the wonderful people who make up the motorcycling community. No matter where you are, they'll come and talk to you and they'll help you out if you need it. I have never worried about being stopped by the side of the road because I know anyone who rides a motorcycle will stop and help me. It's hysterical because I don't know how many times when my kids were small and I was driving them around in the car that I stopped for a stranded motorcyclist who just couldn't believe this little mother was stopping for them.

I love riding. I love the people who ride. I think we have a lot to offer to the community, not just through the fund-raising events, but as a group and individuals. We have a lot to model to our society. We're helpful, supportive and interdependent and that more than anything keeps people riding.

I used to ride to work because it made people realize that, hey, even little old school marms ride motorcycles.

CHAPTER 3

Chariots of Change

"Every time you go out is a new experience and you learn more about the machine and yourself."

—Flight instructor Andrea Tillmann

FOR THE LAST TWO YEARS OF THE CENTURY, I didn't have the time or energy to ride, although my husband had already gotten back into it. Then I went as a passenger on a five-day motorcycle vacation in eastern Ontario. Something was beginning to stir and I had to have another bike. Interestingly, the bike I chose to carry me forward was aptly named: a Honda Shadow Spirit. I soon realized the cruiser style was not quite right for me but it did get me started back on the road to me. My own spirit was beginning to emerge and a motorcycle spirit had arrived to facilitate.

The lesson of the Honda's sprocket is something I still remember vividly. My husband was concerned the engine was revving too high and decided that, in the best interests of me and my Spirit, he would replace the stock rear sprocket with one that was smaller and had fewer teeth. The idea was to reduce the engine revolutions per minute to improve longevity. It also meant I had no get up and go, which

51

frustrated me to no end. If I wanted to pull out and pass, I needed plenty of advance notice to build up a head of steam. I could forget about any extra power on an uphill stretch. It was like regulating my voice and the amount of power available to my spirit.

Other events were unfolding that would test my fledgling return to power. My company was sold, the organization underwent a huge culture shift and I had an opportunity to move into a whole new field, Human Resources. The downside was my new boss, who capped a horrendous transition period by telling me I was a failure. Battered and bruised, with my self-esteem resting at the bottom of the scale, it took considerable courage to persevere but that's exactly what I did. My relationship with my boss remained rocky for the duration of my tenure with the company, but it inured me and taught me to be kind to myself. For that I am thankful.

Overcoming the demands of times like these required male psychic energy. I needed to be focused, assertive, creative and persistent. When I tripped and fell, I knew I'd have to get right back up again. As is always the case, helpers arrived at just the right time: the mentors, role models and others who have gone before, persevered and succeeded. By coming face to face with strength in others, we are able to recognize strength in ourselves.

I was determined to get past this time of turmoil one step at a time. I learned each small success builds on the last one and our strength builds with each successive challenge. Thank God motorcycling was with me once again. The commute through the countryside became therapeutic and I'm not sure how I would have managed without it.

Up to that time in my life, I had disassociated myself from my Mennonite heritage. I never wanted to speak of it or reveal it publicly. I tried to bury that part of my history, which had brought me ridicule, embarrassment and internal strife. Yet in order to let it go, I had to address the fears and guilt bred into me. I hadn't yet seen the value in my heritage, nor recognized it was responsible for my introduction to motorcycling.

My mother had given my husband a book as a birthday gift, *My Harp Is Turned to Mourning*, a history of the German Mennonites in Russia. Now, after the book had been tucked away unread for years, I was suddenly compelled to pick it up and read it. I discovered that, long before my grandmother had hidden the motorcycle behind the false wall, her ancestors were being educated that the end was near and they should repent and conform to avoid eternal damnation. What an eye opener. Nothing had changed. They were so afraid of what was to come after death that they let it rule their lives and missed out on full, joyful living. Fear had ruled my ancestors, just as it was ruling me now.

Another light bulb went on during a visit to the terra cotta warriors in China. Here was an emperor who so feared the afterlife that for his entire lifetime, he conscripted thousands of slaves and artisans to craft intricate, life-sized statues to protect him in his tomb. All of that energy and those resources could have been put to much more productive use. I had seen the same thing at the Egyptian pyramids and at holy sites in India. The epiphany for me was to see that fear of the unknown controlled behavior so often. It wasn't something new with my ancestors. It had been around for thousands of years in many cultures. It didn't make sense. Why not make the best value-based choices every day in my life? Why not be as true to myself as I could and stop letting fear and guilt rule? I was put on the earth to make a positive difference, not to shiver in fear the whole time.

I shared a love of reading with my mentor, the plant manager at my workplace, and we often exchanged books. Since then, a solid friendship has evolved, and so has a relationship that's more like family with Trent, his wife, Patti, and their children and relatives. Incidentally, he had ridden a motorcycle all through university. At the time I'm speaking of, though, I didn't know him all that well yet and I was still pretty meek and mild. One day, I timidly handed him *My Harp Is Turned to Mourning*. This was a huge step for me, the first intentional acknowledgement of my background. I distinctly recall him returning the book to me after he read it. Somehow the hand-off was symbolic of a psychic door opening a little for me. I had exposed my background, spoken openly about it and survived. I now had the courage to start exploring what was inside and figuring out what was calling to get out.

Steadily, my power was returning; the more I discovered I was capable of, the more I wanted to understand how to tap into it. My Honda Spirit had served its purpose and begun my awakening. Now I had to get something better suited to my riding preferences and style.

A Yamaha FZ1 was the perfect choice and it was my companion for more than two hundred thousand kilometers. It had all the power I would ever need and then some. As I pulled away from the dealer, I was terrified I would lose control, but the trepidation was mixed with excitement and my face was beaming. My husband kept warning me about the bike's power and how easily it could get away from me and that I would inadvertently pop a wheelie. Of course, I *was* able to control it. I was beginning to understand it was me who controlled the power.

That bike has taken me on amazing rides and introduced me to people and places I never imagined would be part of my life. But I'm getting ahead of myself. I always had to watch my speed with that bike.

I was also recognizing I was withering in both my marriage and my career. In spite of two years of marriage counseling, it had finally become apparent to me that if I wanted to be true to myself and experience the relationship I craved, firstly with myself, I would have to set out on my own.

The expectations that had gotten me to that point in life had influenced my career choices, too. I had always done all right, but I had never pushed my limits, mired as I was in my lack of confidence, feelings of low self-worth and lack of self-awareness. It's no wonder my work had little meaning for me.

To the observer it appeared I had a rewarding career and a perfect marriage, but I was trying to fill a role that wasn't mine in both of them and it was draining me of my life energy. If my psyche was to remain intact, I would have to make some changes.

Going through the thought process leading up to both decisions was excruciating. I had no idea how I would make it on my own or what lay ahead of me. I knew only that I had to do it, and the longer I waited, the harder it would be.

The talk with my husband was one of the most difficult and heartbreaking conversations I've ever had. I knew how hurt he would be. I kept waiting for the ideal time and setting. There was no easy way and finally, I just did it. I knew without a shadow of a doubt it had to be done so we could both move on.

I moved into my own place in December of 2002. The power I regained through that move gave me the strength to leave my job seven months later.

Part of the reason for my life changes was that I wanted to make a contribution, to leave the world a better place than I found it. I knew I had a lot more potential, and I needed to understand how to access it. It was as though I had discovered a treasure I wanted to share with the world.

I think of it now as a move from a black and white existence to one of vibrant colors and a whole gamut of emotions in a Technicolor world. Then, however, I had yet to learn you can't fully appreciate love, joy and gratitude unless you've experienced fear and angst, too.

When I announced my resignation, I started working with an executive coach. She got me imagining possibilities and asking myself what I really wanted to do. It was a slow process figuring that out. I had to peel back many years of thinking.

Nothing solid came to me but I was able to describe the characteristics of what my next ventures and my ideal relationship would look like. I knew I didn't want a structured job again. Another marriage wasn't on the list either, although I imagined a companion at some point. Above all, I needed to do something meaningful to me personally, where I could leave a legacy.

Not surprisingly, most of my friends, family and business associates questioned my decision to change direction so completely. But then, quietly, individually, they would approach and share their dreams and desires with me.

I began to hear the words "brave" and "courageous" often. To me, though, it would have been riskier for my psyche to stay in the wrong marriage and the wrong career and have them continue to bleed energy away from me. I had become a listless soul inside a shell of myself. I didn't know where I had gone or even who I was, but I intended to become me again.

I also identified another precious gift — two months of riding season with no commitments. I do my best thinking while riding, so the timing couldn't have been better for me to plan a long solo trip.

I didn't see anything really brave about that, either. I had a new, reliable motorcycle and good riding skills. I was healthy and resourceful. I was going to be traveling in Canada and the United States and would have no trouble understanding the language.

The struggle and turmoil I had been going through was something experienced by people throughout history. When the impetus to move forward becomes greater than the urge to resist, we take the step into an empty space between the connections to our past, our identity and our dreams. It's often our time to go alone into the desert, to solicit spirit guides and seek enlightenment.

In *Women Who Run With the Wolves*, poet and psychoanalyst Clarissa Pinkola Estés states: "When women reassert their relationship with their wildish nature, they are gifted with a permanent and internal watcher, a knower, a visionary, an oracle, an inspiratrice, an intuitive, a maker, a creator, an inventor and a listener who guides, suggests and urges a vibrant life in the inner and outer worlds. When women are close to this nature, the fact of that relationship glows through them."[6]

---

[6]   Clarissa Pinkola Estés, *Women Who Run With the Wolves*. Ballantine Books, p.6

The stories in this chapter show the emergence of a part of us that has been hidden and becomes exposed through the motorcycle as a vehicle of change. The key is in the ignition. We turn it on and we hit the starter.

Andrea Tillmann

Occupation: flight instructor
Location: Oakville, Ontario
Age: 48
Riding Discipline: street
Began Riding: 2004

Andrea attended one of my motorcycle maintenance workshops. She was reticent, new to motorcycling, riding a 250 cc Honda Rebel and full of technical questions. Motorcycling entered her life during the upheaval of dealing with a troubled teenager, the breakdown of her marriage and the temporary loss of her commercial pilot's license. Shaken to the core, she found a passion to pick up where flying had left off and complement redefining who she was. Her motorcycle served its purpose and she has since returned to duty.

Exactly when I came to riding is a blur because it was a fairly difficult time in my life. We were having all kinds of problems with one of our sons, and my husband and I finally decided to part after so many unhappy years. I had to go on meds that you're not allowed to fly with, which was a huge loss. As I look back, though, I must have known motorcycling was coming. I had taken a temporary leave from my position as a flight instructor, I went into this dark period over the next six months and then I emerged with my bike license. I can't actually explain what brought me to want to ride other than it came totally from within. I feel now like I'm coming out of the other side of a cyclone. My bike has been a grounding experience for me.

My mom had already thought I was crazy when I started piloting, and she was horrified about the motorcycling and convinced that my father was rolling in his grave. I was the baby of four girls and you just don't do these kinds of things. Actually, my father was thrilled when I started to fly because he had his pilot's license, but he didn't live to see the motorcycle. I was home with Mom a few days ago looking at photographs of me and my motorcycle, and she's beginning to be okay but she's still very skeptical.

My boys are good with me riding and weren't at all surprised when I took it up. Way back when I was learning to fly, they would take my picture for show and tell. They've had a very non-traditional, way-out-there sort of mom for a long time and they're proud of it.

Learning to ride has come naturally for me. The first week or two were really hard, obviously. I started very nervously going up and down my block, and then I would go another block. It was a matter of building my confidence one block at a time and that was a really hard thing to do.

Flying and riding a motorcycle have a lot of similarities. Both are all-consuming mentally and physically. You become totally engrossed. It forces you to focus and concentrate to be safe. It takes everything in you and I love that.

When I started to take my license, I was going to ride a scooter. At the course, we got a small motorcycle that actually had gears, a clutch and the whole bit, and there was no question. I fell in love with the bike rather than just sitting on a scooter and giving it gas. At the time, I was still married, and all the way home I was thinking about how I was going to break this to my husband. I broke it gently and firmly. I wasn't going to ride a scooter and no discussion. He eventually came around.

Another big similarity is the freedom. I get the same feeling on a bike of being in a different world that I used to get in the air. You leave everything behind when you take off. It's probably because it takes everything in you.

Both require a high degree of proficiency in eye-hand coordination. Riding a motorcycle is two-dimensional and flying is three-dimensional, and I miss that, but the bike has answered all the thrill-seeking part of me. I love the technical challenge of riding the bike and maintaining control on challenging roads. Add the smell of fall leaves and the look of beautiful scenery and it feeds my soul.

When I see a woman rider, my reaction is exactly the same as when I see a lady pilot. It is so awesome and I want to get to know them. It takes a lot of courage to ride a bike and a lot of stereotypes are being shattered. It reassures me that we are absolutely equal to men and we can completely do things they can do.

Learning to ride and push your own limits takes a lot of perseverance, drive and courage. It is a very individual thing, just like flying an airplane. It's not like you have a team of people helping you. You really are on your own. You have to dig very deep down and it's you and the bike, just like it was me and the airplane, to figure out any problem. The confidence that grows has spilled over into every area of my life. Even my tennis is better, and in funny ways, it has made me a better mother.

Every time you go out is a new experience and you learn more about the machine and yourself. The first time I rode in the rain, it was very daunting and scary, but I overcame it, and the next day I went out and I'll never forget how confident I felt. You can't help but learn a lot about yourself by how you react to situations. We are all on that journey of learning about ourselves.

During the quiet riding moments, you have uninterrupted time on your own to work things out that you wouldn't be able to do with work demands, the phone ringing and kids running around. It gets you away into a calm, calm place.

Judith Eden

Occupation: retired elementary school teacher
Location: Guelph, Ontario
Age: 65
Riding Discipline: street
Began Riding: 2003

For Judith, learning to ride at age sixty meant revisiting her adolescence and addressing an unfulfilled need. Judith was my first client at Trillium Motorcycle Tours & Events. She asked me to call her Roxanne as soon as we met, referring to it as her "biker name". She came on a number of tours over the years and could always be counted on to add character to any ride. She was determined to be a "biker," and she succeeded, coming to terms with her own persona in the process.

Motorcycles always caught my eye, as did neat-looking cars, and I always liked the outdoors. But most of all, the older I got, the more I realized my adolescence didn't get a chance to be. I'm the eldest of a big family and you have to grow up pretty quickly. Now I wanted a little more risk-taking, a little more fun, a few more dare-devilish things.

I was in a relationship and like a lot of partners, mine was frightened I was going to get hurt if I had a motorcycle, so I didn't buy one for a long time. Then, as I was turning sixty, the relationship busted and I was on my own. I began to wonder if I could capture some of me that I'd put aside and lost.

I took a really good look at myself, at my past and how I wanted to be. I was trying to be a new me after the relationship, moving to a new community and retiring from teaching. It was a new life and I wanted the life to continue to be exciting and positive.

I dropped in one day to a motorcycle shop and was absolutely giddy with wanting what to me as an adolescent had been a toy, albeit a dangerous one. I thought, well, why not?

I took on a whole persona and named her Roxanne. I thought the name was strong and just right for a teenager. We bought the type and color of bike she wanted.

Roxanne was kind of an angry kid because she didn't have enough time to be herself. A motorcycle image can bring that out because it can have that rough, tough edginess to it and Roxanne needed to vent her anger. I needed to say to Roxanne, "We've got to focus this anger in the right way because it could destroy you. We haven't been given a chance for us to grow up and that takes time."

Roxanne picked out her costume and she had a ritual when she got ready to go out riding. We would put on the gloves and the boots and I would get right into it, because if I was trying to be that adolescent, I had to get up out of my own ego self. Judith Eden is a mother and I have to keep myself safe. Roxanne wanted the freedom to go and be on this thing she had always looked at and now owned. Roxanne faced the dangers all the time and said, "Get on that bike and just get out there."

I had never ridden a bike of any sort, and the training sessions were really tough. Then, after the lessons, I got on a different kind of bike and I realized how much bigger and heavier it was. Now I was going to be on the roadways facing cars, too. The mother in me feared for our safety but Roxanne countered with, "We got the bloody bike, we need to follow through" and she was kicking up a fuss. Luckily, I discovered a great big vacant parking lot nearby and I would ride over every day at the least busy times. When I came home I always kissed the motorcycle seat and said, "Thank you. We're here and safe." Building the confidence took a while.

Eventually, I started to go on small group tours and the most fun was when we stopped and stayed in glamorous places. It destroyed stereotypes, because when we pulled up, we were a motorcycle group. There we were, paying for good places to stay that had good wine, getting off a bike after being really gritty all day, going to the pool and then the bar for a martini after. I loved that because it fed my own complexities. Roxanne couldn't go to the bar, but I also have a sophisticated part of me, and even on motorcycle tours I was able to be that person, too. At the end of every one, there was absolute jubilation because I knew what I had accomplished. I would look in the mirror, I would see Roxanne, I would see me, and I would say, "We are heading forward. I'm on a path that, when my days are ended, I'll feel good about myself."

My favorite ride? You never know what the fall is going to be like, so every lovely day is a bonus for a rider, and I said to myself, "Let's just go explore some of the waterfalls in the area." That day was so beautiful and I was on my own for six hours, feeling safe and confident. Six hours just riding around being Roxanne. Everything worked. The bike was functioning well, I didn't feel lost, I wasn't worried, wherever I stopped, people were friendly. Roxanne had a glorious day.

Roxanne and I came together on that ride and I felt a real calmness. That part of me got encompassed with all of me. I had fed my starving adolescent part and she appreciated it. She wasn't crying out for attention anymore.

When I came in from that ride, I was really sore with my shoulder, which had been aggravating me for years, and a knee that was bothering me. I recognized it was time now to take care of another part of me, and I no longer had that craving to ride. It was bittersweet to part from the bike.

I didn't want Roxanne to say, "Now what happens to me?" So I do other things, like rollerblading or dancing. I say, "Okay, Roxanne, let's go out and have some fun."

Diane Ortiz

Occupation: president, Big Apple Motorcycle School
Location: Manhattan, New York
Age: 57
Riding Discipline: street
Began Riding: 1991
Website: www.BigAppleMoto.com

After twenty-one years in an abusive relationship, Diane started life again from scratch. Now motorcycling, teaching others to ride and giving back through motorcycling are the core of her personal and professional activities.

Diane recounted her journey with quiet strength in her voice. Motorcycling played a significant role in her rebirth to life and she has made it her mission to give back, largely through motorcycle-related ventures.

My first taste of riding a motorcycle occurred in my teens. My uncle was a courier for CBS here in New York City and he used to go by motorcycle to the airports to pick up film and photographs coming in by plane. Sometimes on his way back to Manhattan to the networks, he would stop by and sneak me out for a ride. This was the 1960s and riding was a no-no in my family, so I had to put it aside.

I got married, had a family and finally left after twenty-one years of abuse. My husband had sent me to a psychiatrist and for a lot of that time I was sedated. Gradually he isolated me from friends and family. I didn't realize abusers and controllers operate that way.

I took my children with me, but he had visiting rights on the weekend. One weekend he just wouldn't give them back. He had moved a lot of our money to foreign banks and I couldn't touch it. I didn't have the emotional or financial resources to battle him. Sadly, I lost the children.

In 1991, I met a gentleman who was a motorcyclist and he encouraged me to give it a try. I did and I loved it and got my license. My adventure gene was beginning to come alive.

I was very tentative at first. I'm five foot two and I was just learning to control the motorcycle, but I was discovering my own power, too. My friend would question me when I did things like parking where I could get out more easily, but I would tell him, "This is the way I have to do it, and when I'm riding, I'm going to stop where I want to stop. It might not be where you would stop but you just have to accept that."

Sometimes my students are a little tentative themselves. I tell them they have to stand up for themselves. "You're in control of your motorcycle. Don't do something just because somebody else tells you to, whether that means wearing inadequate protective gear or going too fast, going too slow or riding when you don't feel up to riding."

That gentleman, who is now my husband, became an instructor. As my competence and confidence increased, I thought I could do that, too. We both taught part-time at the Motorcycle Safety Foundation for a while.

I had been working at a large newspaper for twenty-seven years, and they offered a buyout. The owner of the school where I had been teaching offered me a job as general manager at a new school he was opening. It turned out, though, that he had done something illegal and had to leave the country. I decided to open my own school.

My husband and I had really old motorcycles and every time we went riding, pieces would fall off, so we didn't want to venture very far from home. In 2001, with our divorces behind us and some savings, it was time for new bikes. That's when I really came alive. I went out with a sport-bike riding group that met online, and ninety-nine percent of the time I was the only woman and I really had to step up. I managed to increase my skills and get better and better. Now a lot of times I'm the one leading the group.

One of my best motorcycle experiences ever was getting on a track and going over one hundred miles an hour. I could be in control, go fast, hang off the bike, enjoy it and feel safe at the same time. There's something about being able to push yourself to find how far you can go and what your limits are and the limits of your motorcycle in a safe environment.

We did a motorcycle trip from San Paulo in Brazil to Rio de Janeiro two summers ago. It was the first time I was in a different country with a different language and it was more challenging than anything I'd ever done so far. The pace was a little bit faster and we faced challenges from the traffic and even from stopping by the side of the road and eating sausages from somebody's little farm stand. Everything was just so different, even riding a motorcycle that's not your own. Our bikes were larger than anything in the area and people weren't used to seeing a woman riding one of that size. I felt like a queen. That just doesn't happen around here unless you look like Barbie or something.

We don't get to do a lot of off-road riding here in New York unless you count the shoulder. The adventure of riding on dirt roads, through the jungle, going places we'd never dreamt of, coming across a little street and having a three-foot vulture sitting there looking at you — it was really exhilarating.

My toughest experiences have been demo rides with strange motorcycles that are very tall and very heavy, especially in uneven terrain where stops are not only on a hill but the road is off-camber and you're leading inexperienced riders. Often I'm doing a review on the bike as well. I've had to kind of make a strategy for myself on a demo ride so I can manage my challenges and the group at the same time. I've overcome the fear of dumping it. That's not the end of the world. Try not to hurt anybody, try not to damage the bike and don't freak out about it.

Motorcycling has made me not afraid to be different. I can forget about anything that's bothering me and just concentrate on riding. In a way that's my way of dealing with things sometimes, and I get the same thing from teaching other people because you're concentrating on them.

It's important to realize, though, that just about anything can empower you, mastering any kind of skill, whether it's beading, or maybe you're a great baker, or something else.

With the school, as I became more independent and more confident, I also became very competitive. I wanted to be good at things. I'd had years and years of being told, "You'll be nothing without me," "No, you can't possibly do your own checkbook. You have to ask me for money." Maybe I went too much the other way.

The friendliness and the camaraderie of other riders helped me come out of my shell a little bit, especially when I was first divorced. It got me through and past the point where other people would ask whether I had kids. At first, I would start to cry. But when you pull up on a motorcycle, nobody asks about kids. They want to know what kind of a bike that is, how long you've been riding and where you are going. Now, I feel that in our own way, through motorcycling and other volunteer activities, we are able to help lots of other people's kids.

Every year, I participate in Race for the Cure's signature event in Manhattan with over ten thousand participants. I also have the honor of putting together a group of women riders to lead everyone into Central Park. A lot of women who are involved in it either know somebody with breast cancer or are survivors themselves or are going through treatment.

Making a difference is what we want to accomplish through our school. The best thing that could happen is that we are touching other people's lives. What's the purpose of living if you're not going to do some good?

Lois Pryce

Occupation: author, journalist, speaker, adventurer extraordinaire
Location: London, England
Age: 36
Riding Discipline: adventure, street
Began Riding: 2002
Website: loisontheloose.com

When motorcycle journalist Adrian Blake heard I was writing this book, he said I had to speak with Lois.

To get the full effect of Lois's spirit and vibrancy, you'll need to read her books, Lois on the Loose *and* White Knuckles, Red Tape, *chronicling her motorcycle adventures through North and South America and Africa.*

Lois was a bored clerical worker at the BBC in London when she decided to take up riding. Suddenly she was a world adventurer. She says anyone can do it.

Almost instantly after passing my motorbike test, I decided to do a big land trip around the world or something similar. I had always had itchy feet. My life was humdrum and uneventful at that point and I used to sit at my desk and dream of adventure.

I'd never done anything like this before and didn't have any special training. I had been riding a motorbike for only a couple of years but I knew a little bit about mechanics. I had never traveled in third world countries and I didn't speak any Spanish. I wasn't some kind of hard-core explorer type at all.

But the hardest thing is just making the decision to go. The scary part is actually making that decision to leave your job, leave your home, leave your family, leave whatever it is and throw yourself into the world and let fate take its course.

Once you're out there, it's actually much easier than you thought it would be. You just get on with it and it doesn't matter who you are, you find a way. And it gives you confidence.

The motorbike plays a big part in defining the adventure because it gives you this sort of image of being different, whether you want it or not. This is even more so in developing countries. Men in South America are often slightly intimidated by a woman rider because she's so alien to them. You get a certain respect that you may not get if you just turn up as part of a tour group on a bus or a back packer or in a car. In a car, you're immediately viewed as being rich. A motorbike in third world countries is a poor man's transport.

You immediately conjure up all these images to observers and, to be honest, it's useful. You're less likely to be taken advantage of or harassed. I saw that every day when I would arrive in a small town or the market on the bike. I'd get off and take off my helmet, and people would be a little bit more wary, a bit more polite. But when I was staying there and I'd walk around in my flip-flops and a sundress, I was being harassed continuously. Unfortunately, in those kinds of situations, the more you act like a man, the better off you are.

When you look back at trips like these, it's the challenges and the dramas that make them worth while. It's almost as though if everything went really easy and according to plan, it wouldn't be as satisfying an experience. There's a pleasure in using your initiative and your resourcefulness to get out of sticky situations. Occasionally, I would have those "what the hell am I doing" moments. But then I would think, well, would I rather be here in wherever, Mexico, El Salvador, Congo, on my motorbike, having this experience, even though things were at that moment going wrong, or would I rather be sitting in the office, back in London? The answer at the time, no matter *what* was going on, was always yes, I would rather be here. That's the case when my bike's broken down or it's freezing cold or it's raining or I'm lost. Or maybe you've had a run-in with some local because they've tried to rip you off or you've been roughed up by the police.

Often people would comment on how courageous I was, especially local women who had never been outside of their own village. I would always say they could do it, too. Because that is the message. I don't like these myths that it's only for the big boys and the tough. I'm a normal person, five feet four inches and not particularly strong. I'm not rich. I don't know people in important places in embassies or anything like that. If I can do it, anybody can do it.

I get so many emails from women who say they want to learn to ride but their boyfriends or husbands or dads won't let them or don't think they should. Everyone tells them it's dangerous. That's my greatest beef, this whole dangerous thing. I've ridden around all these places and I'm still in one piece. Just because something has an element of danger isn't a reason not to do it.

Chantal Cournoyer

Occupation: manager of marketing, promotions and events at
Harley-Davidson Montréal/ Moto Internationale BMW Motorrad
Location: Montreal, Quebec
Age: 41
Riding Experience: street, off-road, dual-sport, adventure
Began Riding: 1992

*For several years, I've worked with BMW Motorrad Canada to coordinate
their Ontario Exclusively Ladies Demo Female Test Ride Events. Through that
involvement, I was invited to participate in BMW Motorrad Summerfest,
a popular event at Mosport International Raceway.*

*Chantal attends annually, representing her dealership and offering rider
training. I've been impressed by how someone so small in stature could
so skillfully and confidently maneuver large, powerful motorcycles with
high seat heights, particularly at slow speeds.*

Last year, a woman came into the Harley-Davidson boutique I
manage and talked about *Trophée Roses Des Sables,* a rally for women
in the Moroccan desert, which she had completed with a four-by-
four. What was planted in my mind was the challenge of doing it on
motorcycles with my friend Stephanie.

The goal of the rally is to cover the shortest distance possible,
using only a rule book and a compass. Our goal wasn't to win. It was
to participate, to finish it with a bike that wasn't broken and to have
fun. We were the first ever to complete it on motorcycles.

Riding it on a bike was a completely different experience than
in a four-by-four. For example, when it was hailing, we had to stop
because it was hurting our faces. Then it rained for two days, so not
only were the river beds flooded, but the trails between them were

full of water, too. In order to cross the rivers, we had to push through strong currents in waist-deep water with the bikes in first gear.

One day, Stephanie tried to start her bike again after a stop and it wouldn't start. We tried and tried. After an hour, Stephanie insisted I continue and she would wait for help. We were both in tears, but the team we were with and I finally left her with food and water under a tree near a couple of houses and gave her a sweater in case it took a while for help to arrive. After traveling a few kilometers, all of a sudden we noticed Stephanie approaching from behind us. She had removed a side panel and touched a wire and the bike started again. We were all ecstatic, especially her.

It took a lot of determination to get through. I would give myself pep talks and say, "Okay, Chantal, let's go. You can do it. It's all inside your head." I know Mom was with me during that trip because I was speaking to her. Stephanie thought the same thing about her father. We had our own angels. Also, there was a truck with a medical guy and driver, and the organization told them, always keep an eye on the two motorcyclists. We said they were our angels, too.

At one point, I dropped my bike in a sand dune around nine p.m. after we'd been riding since five-thirty a.m. I had pulled a butt muscle and it was very painful. I couldn't lift the bike alone, so when I dropped the bike I screamed, "I'm tired. Do you understand? I'm tired and what are we doing here?" The stress had to get out. Stephanie came over with her kind words and she calmed me and relaxed me. It happened twice and had to get out, but afterward it was OK.

At the Marrakesh hotel where the closing gala evening was held, we came down the stairs to the hall in the middle of screaming and applause. We tried to figure out what that was all about. It turned out it was for us. We didn't win but we received a standing ovation.

Riding gives me confidence, you meet a lot of nice people, and my life is full. In the summer, I do a lot of off-road riding and camping with friends.

When I get together with old friends — sometimes you look at people and you think they have a boring life, and for me it's so different.

Cheryl Stewart

Occupation: freelance sculptor and scenic artist, and creates
sculptural scenery for theatre, film and television
Location: Manhattan, New York
Age: 41
Riding Discipline: street
Began Riding: 1981
Website: http://home.bway.net/cstewart/

*Cheryl chose motorcycling deliberately because it meant going against
the grain and symbolized a new beginning. More than twenty-five years
later, she considers it an entry into many places and things. She commutes
daily through the potholes of Manhattan. Her aggressive riding style,
belied by her soft demeanor, has earned her a reputation for actually
wearing out her motorcycles, and it takes some doing to be stronger
than your machines.*

In 1981, as a teenager, I moved from New York City, where I
had grown up, to San Francisco for a year and a half. I wanted to
do every fun thing that usually only boys got to do. Back then, even
in San Francisco, it was revolutionary, subversive and shocking for
a woman to ride a motorcycle. I think one of the reasons was that
most women then were somehow afraid of not appearing feminine
enough, even for the lesbians. Straight women thought they would
turn men off by being too masculine, so riding was off limits. I feel
as though, even back then, I was a role model, because women would
see me and say, "She's no bigger than I am and she's riding. I could
do that, too." We looked like we were having fun. Within a month
of getting my license, I was on the first of many big cross-country
motorcycle trips.

I'm notorious for going through bikes. It's because I ride really
hard and aggressively in New York City and I also take the same bike

to the track. It's hard to convey how intense an experience riding
around New York City is unless you've been here. We have a lot of
potholes and very aggressive drivers, and you're constantly on and off
the throttle. I actually broke the suspension on my motorcycle going
through a pothole this spring.

I really love the intangible benefits, that feeling I get of power,
control and absolute mastery of the machine. People have been writing about it for a long time and I don't think anyone captures it very
well. Non-riders talk all the time about the dangers of riding and they
rarely talk about the benefits. That's not to say it couldn't happen.
Life has made me very aware the worst things can indeed happen.
To me it's more than well worth it. I was so deeply troubled when I
was younger and the pure joy I get from riding is one of the things
that kept me alive. If I didn't ride, I might not have lived this long,
so the rest is gravy.

When I ride, I experience those remarkable feelings of mastery,
joy and thrill. If you don't have enough of that in your life, and you're
deeply troubled, sometimes you might not want to stick around any
longer. If you know that you have this to look forward to, that you
can do this thing that makes you so happy, well then, you're not in
any danger of checking out early.

From the day I started riding, I took safety pretty seriously, but I
still always wanted to take the experience to the very edge, because it
was fun. If you start riding as a younger person, you have all of that
kind of exuberance and feeling of invincibility, which makes riding
incredibly thrilling, but also much more dangerous. It sets up a pattern in your life that, wow, I can do this! People who start later start
with much heavier burdens and so much more to lose.

I've always ridden hard. I'm very fit, muscular and limber and
I've fallen down many times. I'm not proud of this but I have —
and I get up and walk away. I didn't have any serious repercussions
until 2002, when I was struck from behind as I pulled my disabled

motorcycle over to the shoulder on a major highway on the east side of Manhattan.

That was a rude awakening. I had thought I was aware something bad could happen, but I found out I hadn't really believed it anymore. At about the same time, two other friends were injured in accidents. The following spring, my partner, who had been riding only a couple of years, was hit by somebody going through a stop sign. She died instantly. We make our choices and it never crossed my mind not to ride after any of these accidents.

I love the absolute freedom of free-form trips. I wake up in the morning and I choose a direction, which I can change at any time. I find a really nice, private spot to camp with a pond or a stream. When I wake up in the morning, the birds are singing, the fish are jumping and it's really quite extraordinary to be answering to no one. It's about riding around and experiencing whatever comes and I love that kind of adventure. I haven't done that in a while. I'm older now and life's a little different, but I feel another one coming on. After my partner's accident, it's taken me a while to get back.

What we don't realize as bikers is that by having fun and doing this thing where your reaction time is really important, we are exercising something other people don't. Discipline is really important to keeping a sharp mind as we age. Since I've started doing a lot more track days, my reaction time started climbing again — in my forties.

Motorcycling is very meditative, particularly riding through New York City traffic, believe it or not. You can't be attached to any one moment. You can't be angry that someone beeped somebody. In any moment, you really have to practice detachment and finding ways around difficult situations. Something undesirable can happen if you become attached to your spot in the lane that someone's infringing on. That's a good spiritual practice for anyone in any life.

I often do my best thinking while I'm riding. As you're traveling, you move forward, and to me it's a way to send your mind forward at the same time. My mind is traveling, my motorcycle is traveling.

If there's something I have to puzzle through, it's much easier to do on a motorcycle than anywhere else.

Riding is an entry to so many places and things. I'm conspicuous at the jobs I get to and everybody knows who I am. I've met people through motorcycling I would never have had access to otherwise. I have so many things I wouldn't have had if I hadn't started to ride. We really have to start talking about these things that are so beneficial.

I'm now a track-day instructor at Fish Tail Riding School in Loudon, New Hampshire. I also coach the novice rider groups for the Sirens Women's Motorcycle Club. I feel it's good to support new riders and I'm glad I can do that in that way.

To me, it's a simple risk/rewards equation and the risks don't come anywhere near outweighing the rewards. Maybe one day I will put my leg over the bike and think the risks really do outweigh the rewards. I just don't think that day is coming any day soon, if at all.

CHAPTER 4

Getting Past Go

*"Motorcycling has transferred knowledge and the strength of
never-give-up to me. You just assess the situation, turn the
negative into the positive and keep going. This is how I live
my life. And this is how I've taken every single step of my life
adventure."*

—211 MX School owner Stefy Bau

I MOVED INTO A LOVELY apartment that, like the house I had left,
was in the country, surrounded by hardwood forest and set well
back from the road. It was in the basement, but had a walkout to
the gardens, windows on two sides and a cozy fireplace. It was very
tranquil and just what I needed for rejuvenation. I even had a special
stall in the garage for my motorcycle. The seclusion and the fact that
a significant portion of it was surrounded by earth made it seem like
a safe haven. It was like going back to the womb for a rebirth. And
now it was time to poke my head out.

On August 4th, 2003, at 2:52 p.m., two days before my grandmother's birthday, I pulled out of my driveway and was off. I had
actually planned to leave on August 2nd but a migraine sidelined me

for two days. I'm sure it was caused by stress and fear, even though I was excited to be leaving. Even the day I left, I had a small bout of stage fright and had to give myself a nudge to actually get going. Here I was, forty-eight years old, with no job, no income, no prospects, newly single and embarking on a two-month cross-country solo motorcycle trip. I was heading into the unknown geographically and metaphorically and had a whole blank slate in front of me, waiting for me to write the script.

I was following a path through the chaos and ultimately would have to let go of behaviors, thoughts and beliefs that not only no longer served me, but also hindered my progress. The trick would be to recognize fears that were creating resistance, identify self-limiting beliefs and destroy them one by one, rather than let them continue to hold me away from who I was.

Starting with small successes would help reclaim some strength and provide more energy for the next challenge. I understood I could gain power with each incremental success, which could then be used for moving forward rather than just overcoming resistance. Looking at the whole picture was too daunting, but if I took one day at a time, it was manageable. I had two months where every day, I was going for a motorcycle ride. I could handle that.

Included in my luggage was a bag of wool skeins. I was knitting an afghan for my young nephew along the way, weaving my thoughts and experiences into a blanket that would one day provide comfort to him. I did, however, take a lot of ribbing for it. Biking, a solo adventure and knitting seemed like an incongruous combination to my friends.

Right from the start, everyone I met on my trip was hospitable, generous and kind. A few doubts cropped up in my mind on the second morning about whether I could physically handle the trip but by noon they were history. As I headed north from Sault Ste. Marie through the spectacular scenery along Lake Superior, I felt myself lifting out of the consumerism, smog and madness of southern Ontario and the life I was leaving behind.

By day three, I was flying west along the Trans-Canada Highway, the sun was smiling, a huge weight was gone. Time and again I found myself throwing my left hand in the air and yelling "Yahoo!!" in my helmet. That's the beauty of a full-face helmet. You can scream at the top of your lungs and no one hears you.

After visiting my sister in Winnipeg for a few days, I headed northwest to Dalmeny, Saskatchewan, a small farming community north of Saskatoon, to visit the homestead where my mother was born. This trip was about discovering how I came to be, what made me who I was and understanding those ingrained hidden fears I had allowed to control my life.

My grandfather's oldest brother had worked for International Harvester in China and was able to borrow the money from his employer to get the rest of his family out of Russia. My grandparents landed in Quebec City in 1924. Canadian Pacific Railway took them and twenty thousand other Mennonites out west at no charge. They paid back every cent of the fare over time.

My grandparents joined the Schultzes, a Mennonite family in Dalmeny, Saskatchewan, who took them in as farm labor and gave them a place to call home. Over the years, our families remained in touch and I knew the homestead was still owned by Schultzes.

Mr. and Mrs. Schultz, both in their nineties, greeted me warmly. He had been a child when my grandparents arrived but he remembered them well.

Other than the huge combines and agricultural equipment in the yard, the farmhouse looked exactly as it did in the pictures from over eighty years ago. I wondered what thoughts went through my grandparents' minds as they came up the driveway in a landscape that must have been very similar to the one they had left behind. Their faith and strength of spirit was part of who I was. My life changes were a drop in the ocean in comparison.

I was a little concerned that crossing the prairies would eventually turn to drudgery. It was quite the opposite. I loved the vastness and openness. The sky, the fields and the dreams went on forever. I and my motorcycle were completely absorbed in the landscape and savored the prairie beauty as we moved through it. I visited Michichi, Alberta, where my grandparents had bought their own land and persevered through three crop failures before moving to Ontario in 1931, still with nothing more than the clothes on their backs and, by then, three young children.

On the way across the prairies, I visited a number of aboriginal interpretive centers, including the Wanuskewin Heritage Park in Saskatoon and a display at the Glenbow Museum in Calgary. I was fascinated by the simple lifestyle depicted and the connection to and respect for nature. It seemed sad these cultural values had been so lost, but the message from hundreds of years ago resonated with me. My life was so far removed from the basics, the connection to who I was had almost been lost. Now I was finding it again.

That year was a particularly destructive forest-fire season in the Rockies, and most of the time I was in the area the air was thick with acrid smoke. I cut my visit to Banff short because I couldn't see even the mountains the town was nestled in. The road I wanted to take over to British Columbia had been closed because of the fires but reopened that very morning as I prepared for departure. A pilot vehicle was required to guide us through because only one lane was navigable and the fire was still being actively fought around us.

Traveling by motorcycle offers some advantages, including being first on and off ferries. This time, I was courteously moved to the front of the line behind the pilot truck. The other vehicles would have kicked up a lot of ash into my face.

I was awed by the enormity of the devastation on either side of me. Blackness and smoldering posts stood where lush green forests had thrived only days ago. The only color came from the orange buckets swinging from the bellies of helicopters as they moved water to extinguish the flames.

And then, out of nowhere, a stream appeared at the side of the road, with water rushing over the rocks, carrying with it the seeds of regeneration. Here in the middle of blackness and destruction, new life was already starting. The stream didn't stop because of a fire. It kept doing what it always did in being true to its nature. It just went about its business as usual. Life goes on and we move forward.

The redwood forest in northern California was another landmark experience. Riding through the tunnel created by the canopy of those majestic giants, I wondered what they had seen in their lifetime. Inhaling the redwood scent, feeling the damp coolness and admiring the unwavering strength of the forest, I was overcome with awe. I had to stop and absorb it. I spent the night in a beautiful hostel, backed into the redwoods and facing the Pacific. It just doesn't get much better than that.

Frequently the words "brave" and "courageous" came up in conversation about my solo motorcycle journey with both men and women I met along the way. I didn't see it that way, but others did. I sensed a message here for my next line of work. The thought would surface and then I'd park it, hoping it would crystallize as time went on.

That happened a few weeks later. I was visiting my friends Trent — the same plant manager I exchanged books with a few years previously — and his wife, Patti, who were now living near San Francisco. During dinner on an outdoor patio my last evening there, we struck up a conversation with the couple at the next table. The subject of my trip came up and again the words "brave" and "courage" crept in. I said again it was no big deal to me. The woman pointed out that "if that many people are telling you something, you should be listening."

The penny dropped. I would create a business around motorcycles, focusing on women riders but not exclusively, facilitating experiences that would inspire confidence and personal growth. My mind was settled. I could return.

I think my parents had given up hope of trying to understand what had happened to the daughter they knew. To them, I was a different person. But they always, even in their bewilderment, offered unconditional love and support. When I got back from my trip, Mom, searching for the right words, asked: "Did you find your purpose?" It was like it had been hiding under a rock somewhere, maybe in the mountains or on the prairies.

Although the trip was quite an adventure, it was only the beginning. My self-awareness had increased, but years of fear-based decision making don't go away in two months.

The stories in this chapter depict experiences where the women were no longer satisfied with the status quo in their lives. Something inside of them was calling them to step outside of their comfort zone. Intuitively, they knew they had to take this step to continue flourishing, frightening as it might seem at the time. They not only stepped out, but they persisted with dogged determination, through physical, emotional and mental barriers. Each one succeeded and went on to reap the rewards.

Patti Pepin

Occupation: legal assistant
Location: Hamilton, Ontario
Age: 54
Riding Discipline: street
Began: 2005

I met Patti when she signed up for one of our tours. She was fifty years old and had never had a car license, but here she was, a grandmother, riding a motorcycle. You can imagine it wasn't easy for her to learn. In fact, she was told during the course to hang up her helmet. But she had a brand new motorcycle at home, waiting for her. Since the instructor told Patti she wasn't meant to be a rider, she's enjoyed thousands of solo kilometers.

Two years ago, on her way to the Yukon for the summer solstice, she slid off the road and broke her right shoulder. Strangely, we ended up seeing the same supportive leading orthopedic surgeon. After one of my appointments, I stopped at a local bike shop and, during a conversation with the sales rep, learned the used FZI sitting on the lot, the exact model as mine, belonged to another woman. I found out later Patti had purchased it, minutes after being cleared by the doctor.

Like so many women of my generation, I started out on the back of a partner's motorcycle. My first ride, even as a passenger, was at the age of forty-nine, when I started dating a rider. I was terrified for the first half hour and then I was hooked. Part of what I felt even riding on the back was a connection to everything around me. It brought back memories and the same kind of carefree, relaxed feeling I experienced as a kid when I lived on a bicycle from dusk to dawn. But the relationship didn't last, so I'd have to give up on the whole thing, meet someone else I could ride with or learn to ride myself.

I've always hated being in a car, even as a passenger, and have never had a desire to learn to drive, so the decision to learn to ride surprised even me. I fell in love with a shiny red Burgman 400 and promptly plunked down the money about a week before my course.

I was horrible. I kept stalling the bike and didn't even make it through the first day. The instructor tried to console me by saying some people weren't meant to ride motorcycles or bicycles and I should be proud of even trying. I still remember so vividly walking home from the course, carrying my helmet and jacket, crying all the way.

Still in tears when I got home, I told my daughter what the instructor had said. She pointed out I hadn't been hurt and I hadn't hurt anyone else. Secondly, I could not only ride a bicycle, it was my main method of transportation. My Burgman was an automatic, so I didn't have to get really good at shifting, just enough to pass my test.

The following Monday, I booked another course. Getting that license was my proudest riding moment. August 21, 2005.

I quickly upgraded my scooter to a Kawasaki ZR, which took me more than sixty thousand kilometers over the next two years. I've taken three off-road riding courses and spent a day at the racetrack — always the oldest person at both venues.

When you start, you have to think and you have to concentrate. Then one day you're out there and you don't feel anymore where you end and the bike begins.

Because I didn't drive, the change was much bigger for me than for a lot of people. Before, unless I was going with someone or on a bus, I didn't travel. I could fly someplace but once I was there, I couldn't really explore all the little nooks and crannies and anywhere outside the general area where I got deposited. So, learning to ride really opened a lot of things for me.

In 2006, I was navigating a beautiful curve in Vermont en route to the Americade motorcycle rally and momentarily took my eyes off of where I was going. I slid off the road and along the grass. I promised myself that if I walked away from this, I would never get on a motorcycle again.

The fates decided otherwise. The nursing staff didn't want to cut off my gear. They wanted to preserve it so I could use it again. By the time my daughters came to pick me up and we started home, it felt all wrong. There were motorcycles everywhere. I don't belong in this car; I belong out there with you guys. I'm one of you. I want to go back!

One daughter and a lot of other people strongly encouraged me to return to riding. My boss said, "You've become such a different person since you started riding your motorcycle, and I mean that only in a good way. It would be a shame for you to give it up."

A couple of months later, when the orthopedic surgeon was done with me, I asked him if I could ride again. He said everybody has to have something in their lives they love — a far different perspective from when I broke my wrist roller-blading and that surgeon told me he never wanted to see me on roller blades again. I thought, well, tell me where you'll be and I'll make sure not to skate there.

Less than three hours after I saw this latest surgeon, I was in the motorcycle shop. I thought it would be prudent to stick with a 125 cc model and then decided on a cruiser. The salesperson was closing the sale when another customer came by and said, "You can't sell her that! It's not her!" I rode away on a gently used Yamaha FZ1.

My confidence was tested shortly after that. I followed my GPS on a paved road that turned to gravel and kept deteriorating. The next thing I knew it was full of potholes and water. The memory of going down was still pretty fresh. I started to get just a little panicky until my off-road training kicked in. I calmed myself down, relaxed. I remembered, don't do anything sudden, stay off the front brake and get your weight up on your pegs. I told myself, "You know the bike will bounce around but you'll be fine." Once through, I pulled my bike off to the side and reset my GPS to avoid gravel roads.

So many little things have come about from riding. What really stands out when I think about it all is just how much I've learned about myself. I've never done anything before where the desire to do it really overrode all the obstacles, even the accident and being injured, and then being scared and nervous getting back on. But whatever I get from riding has been stronger than all the obstacles. It defies logic. Logic tells you that you're doing something that's dangerous, you've already had an accident and you're not getting any younger.

There is such a sense of community and belonging out there. Even traveling alone, you're never alone. Any place you stop and there's a bike, you've got someone to have a coffee or a conversation with.

Sometimes I'm out there and I'll get this great big grin on my face and think, "I'm riding a motorcycle?" Even after all these kilometers. "This isn't me. I don't ride motorcycles. I take the bus."

Jolene Mosca

Occupation: business development, employee benefit
consulting firm
Location: Hamilton, Ontario
Age: 50
Riding Discipline: street
Began Riding: 1993

Jolene weighed three hundred pounds when she was thirty-five years old. She had always wanted to ride and it became her reward for reaching her goal weight.

Neither losing the weight nor learning to ride afterward came easily, but she succeeded with both. Learning she had that power within her increased her confidence and self-esteem. Challenging herself, getting out on longer tours and experiencing the desert by motorcycle raised her awareness even further.

It made such a symbolic difference in her life that she made a conscious decision to become a mentor to other women learning to ride. She calls herself a mother hen. An annual weekend event she organizes for a group of friends is the highlight of their riding season.

When I met Jolene, her openness, her smile, her effervescent personality and her warmth made me forget the cold winds blowing outside.

At the age of sixteen, I desperately wanted to ride a Harley. It had to be a Harley. Of course at sixteen, that was almost impossible and it took me until I was thirty-five to get it.

In 1991, I weighed three hundred pounds. I started Weight Watchers and promised myself that if I got to my goal weight, I was going to buy myself that Harley. And I did. I got to my goal weight in January, 1993, and that June I bought myself my first Harley and got my license.

That's how I started riding. And it has been my therapy. When I'm stressed, when I have problems in my life, I get on my bike, I go out in the country and I lose myself. I do find that very invigorating and empowering.

I lost my mother in 1989. Growing up, I always heard her saying, "If I ever catch you on a motorcycle …" Well, you can imagine. She passed away in 1989 and the money she left was how I was able to buy my motorcycle. Even after the course, I limited myself to parking lots for a while, doing my figure eights. Everyone would tease me. "Are you ever going to get on the real road?" "Are we ever going to see this motorcycle?" I vowed one of my first rides would be to the cemetery, which it was. The first time my father saw me on this thing, my corners were still horrendous because they took practice. He shut his eyes. He was scared. "Are you sure you want to do this?" And, "Why are you doing this?" I mastered it because I wanted to.

At first, I was a nervous wreck. I thought, "What the hell did I do?" It wasn't feeling like I thought it was going to feel. I was scared to death. My palms were sweaty and I was shaking. But I also remember when I mastered right-hand turns and how I felt. YES!!!!!! I was the worst right-hand turner ever. I'd always be into the oncoming traffic lane. Then came that feeling of accomplishment the first time I actually did it the way you're supposed to. One more thing learned.

It took a few years until I became what I call one with the bike. The first couple of years I was sitting on top of it, operating it and going through the motions. When I became one with the bike, that's when I said, "*This* is what it's supposed to feel like. This is what I *thought* it was going to feel like." In the beginning it was nothing like that. It was work.

I kept at it because I wanted it so bad. When I would see somebody on television, it would look so cool. It looked like it would be a freedom feeling, and I finally reached that.

In 1996, when I'd been riding for only three years, I was in Daytona for Bike Week with some friends. They said, "C'mon, let's ride on the beach." I thought, oh man, this is going to be like in the movies. This is going to be great! Well, it wasn't. The tide had just gone out, the sand was wet, it was like you were riding on grease. I was screaming and yelling the whole time. "This is not like the movies! Get me off of here!"

I absolutely love riding in the desert. It's so wide open and free. I love riding without a helmet and you can do that in the desert. My husband and I did a wonderful trip in Arizona, South Dakota and Colorado and we said, "I could definitely live like this. All that stuff we have in the house is stuff." I couldn't imagine doing that trip in a car. You don't get the same wide-open feeling.

I also love big groups and riding with the girls — the high, the rush, the power. About twenty of us get together every September for a weekend ride. One year we were riding through a small beach town and I remember a guy yelling, "Oh my God, they're all chicks!!" I was inside my helmet going, YES!!!

A core group of about ten of us have been together for almost seventeen years and we've developed this incredible bond. We've been through everything together: divorce, death, disease. We've lost two girls through cancer. It seems that each year, one of us will be going through something life-changing and we're always there to support each other. We've all grown older in a good way. We've matured. We've talked about this amongst ourselves and how conversations have changed. Why we get together has changed. It has taken a shift for the positive and it's wonderful.

We used to get together only once a year, in September. Now we meet countless times throughout the year. Last year, for my fiftieth birthday, one friend had a bunch of the girls here for me. We had a nice party and brought in an esthetician to get our nails done and a pedicure. It's absolutely amazing how strong the bond is and it's all through riding. We wouldn't know each other without that common thread. We're all so different. We come from very different walks of life, we're all different ages, which makes it really nice for the young women, to have the older women to look up to as role models. Underlying it all is this amazing respect and admiration for each other.

I'm like an old mother hen to them and I organize the entire get-together weekend, including a place to stay that can accommodate all of us. We don't want to do all the cooking anymore so now I've got a caterer.

Before I started riding myself, for one season, I rode on the back of the bike of a fellow I was dating. We were on a charity poker run and met a mutual friend and her husband, both riders. I remember to this day exactly what she was wearing. I looked at her with awe and said, "I would *love* to be like *her*. Look at her!" She became my mentor and we became very good friends. She is one of the reasons I am riding today, because she helped me over some hurdles. Now I can be that mentor to other women riders.

It wasn't accepted or the norm for so many years for women to ride. And it still isn't. How many guys would say to me over the years, "Whose bike is that?" I'd respond, "It's my bike." "It's yours???" So we're getting there, but it's still not there. It's good to see another woman, another woman, another woman riding. Maybe the rest of the world will get it one day. Yes, we can do this.

Cathy Walter

Occupation: regulatory affairs professional
Location: Bolton, Ontario
Age: 50
Riding Discipline: street
Began: 2004

When I first met Cathy, she was terrified but determined to learn to ride. She had purchased a new 750 Honda Shadow but was so fearful even I didn't know how she got through it unscathed.

We lost touch and then reconnected a few years later at a motorcycle event. What a difference! She had found others to ride with at a local HOG (Harley Owners Group) Chapter, and now she has ridden through the eastern states and all of Ontario, and out to the West Coast. Most of the guests at her wedding earlier this year came from her riding circles.

A brief stint as a passenger appealed to my sense of adventure and I decided to get my license. Although the relationship ended shortly after, my desire to learn to ride did not. Even my spectacular fall off the bike during the course didn't deter me, and I passed. I purchased my first bike the following spring and then got scared.

A friend tried to help by taking me out for rides, but it only made matters worse. Maybe it was because I was riding second in formation, but I kept looking at the side of the road and thinking I was going to go into the gravel.

I was paralyzed. I was stuck. But I really wanted to learn to ride. I searched the Internet for someone to teach me. All I could find were courses in a parking lot, and I'd mastered that. I reached out to Mark Richardson, Editor of the Wheels section at the Toronto Star. He recommended I contact a local college.

One of the instructors lived nearby, and he came over to my house. He said he wanted to see me ride down the street, so I rode a block, turned around and came back. "Now go down there," he said, pointing in the opposite direction. I was terrified. "No. I never go that way. I only go this way." He turned my bike around, took me out a couple of times and got me feeling a little bit better.

Before I even bought my first bike, I joined a HOG Chapter to meet other riders. Every Friday, I would take the day off and a friend from the club would go out riding with me. I kept hoping for a red light, just so I could put my feet down, but the lights were always green. I couldn't stop and of course he *wouldn't* stop, so I had to keep going. I would look at the gravel shoulder, panic would try to surface and I'd struggle to refocus on riding.

He told me the whole idea of pulling up at a stoplight is so you can have a little chat with the rider next to you. He also tried to instruct me on the fine art of waving to other riders. But that would have meant releasing my death grip on the handle bars, and there was no way I was going to do that.

I can't count the number of times I got off my bike and said I was never going to get on again. I'd just get a tow truck to bring the bike home and then sell it. Yet, when you're having a good day on the bike, it feels so wonderful. I didn't want to give that feeling up, or succumb to defeat.

One day, the route of a club ride went out to a town about an hour from my home before we stopped for lunch. As we were leaving, our ride captain realized he didn't know the area, so he didn't know the way to my home, either. I knew exactly where I was going and offered to lead.

That was my turning point. I had always needed an escort to my door, but here I was leading the group! Since then, I've had many more wonderful rides, and I've ridden all over North America. Riding has given me so much confidence in myself. My outrageous fear wasn't based on anything that had happened to me. I had just viewed the motorcycle as a big machine that was really hard to figure out and kept telling myself I couldn't manage it.

Learning to ride was a vivid reminder that I hadn't challenged myself in a while, and now it was time for a new challenge. If nothing else, when you can get past those irrational thoughts and focus on believing in yourself, you can enjoy everything and everyone else around you that much more.

Teresa Vincent

Occupation: self-employed airbrush/graphic artist
Location: Barrie, Ontario
Age: 38
Riding Discipline: street
Began Riding: 2000
Website: ucabranding.com

Teresa is proud that she challenges mainstream ideas. She has answered the call to adventure in numerous ways throughout her life.

I met her through the Suzie Q ride, a charity ride for women that she founded in honor of her mother to help find a cure for breast cancer.

I airbrushed motorcycles before I ever rode them. I was probably twenty-three or twenty-four at the time and I was airbrushing leathers for a husband and wife who each had their own motorcycle. The woman asked why I didn't ride. I had never thought of it. I actually ended up buying her motorcycle, a big old cruiser. My mom, still in shock, followed me in a vehicle and kept saying, "I can't believe that's my daughter on that motorcycle."

In 2000, my mom was re-diagnosed with cancer and I wanted to do something to help out, so I started the Susie Q Ride. I also needed an outlet for all the stress and fear. Miraculously, she actually attended the very first Susie Q ride and waved the start flag. Motorcycling was not her thing at all, but that's just another example of how amazing she was, because she was really supportive in everything I did. I'm glad Mom was able to be a part of it for the first year. Her sister is a cancer survivor and she has attended the events since my mom died. They actually took chemo together, believe it or not. Coffee and chemo on Tuesdays.

We've had seven events and raised close to sixty thousand dollars for our local cancer treatment facility. I take flack every year because it's a ride for women only, but we want to keep it unique. We want a safe, welcoming environment. We understand that, for new women riders, learning to ride is an astronomical accomplishment and it's not every day they get to attend a ride that's not intimidating, where women can learn how to group ride and learn how to do it safely.

Shannonville racetrack was the location for my absolute favorite experience on the motorcycle. You get in your groove and you're pushing the limits. I also absolutely love riding through the mountains. That takes you away completely and is more of a meditation.

My most challenging ride was a seven-day trip to Mount Washington in the White Mountains. It was cold and rained solid the whole time. It wears you down and it's exhausting. Coming home, it was still rainy, foggy and extremely cold, and you're sitting on the bike for hour after hour after hour. You're afraid that if you hit a stoplight and you actually have to put your foot down, your leg's not going to move because it's frozen.

We passed a motorcycle accident that put a worse chill in the air, and we rode back with really heavy hearts.

Since then, I've learned a lot about packing appropriately and also how the right gear can make or break it. I now have a heated jacket and extra gear that makes life much more comfortable in bad weather.

The lessons from motorcycling permeate through everything. Pretty much everything I accomplish or strive for in life is not on a mainstream path, something I'm really proud of. I don't know how it turned out like this or why, but I'm glad.

Riding gives us a real sense of inner strength and the awareness that we're capable of more than either other people or even we ourselves think we can do. I think it says a lot about someone's personality and what they're able to accomplish.

People's interests are displayed in the artwork they put on their bikes. If someone's into dragons, then that's what they're going to put on their bike. It's like an extension of them and very heartfelt.

Having said that, I have a black bike with no artwork on it. Completely stock paint. I'm the most indecisive person on the planet and I can do artwork for everyone else without a problem. When it comes to my own, I just can't pick a subject. I do not know what I want on my bike.

I've completely evolved as a rider. I've gone from a cruiser, to a cruiser with more chrome and bigger, louder pipes, to the big obnoxious bike, and now I've evolved into sport touring and won't go back. I consider myself to have matured, going from the big, flashy bike to the functional bike with no artwork on it. I think there's an evolution in everything and that's expressed in your bike, too.

Hazel Carson

Occupation: senior career transition consultant
Location: Brampton, Ontario
Age: 61
Riding Discipline: street
Began Riding: 1997

Hazel works with people changing careers and has found that riding a motorcycle helps her connect with her clients. She has held executive positions throughout her career and is used to setting high standards and succeeding. She laughs when she recalls thinking she'd be able to ride a Gold Wing as a starter bike. She rides one like a pro now and has enjoyed thousands of kilometers on it throughout Canada and the United States.

Learning to ride a motorcycle was the hardest thing I ever did. Not intellectually, because it wasn't hard to learn the theory. Everything else was hard about it — physically hard, emotionally hard, mentally hard.

We spent our honeymoon on a Gold Wing on Manitoulin Island, with me riding around on the back. Once when we went down to the Americade rally, we had stopped somewhere by the side of the road to have a snack and three people on Gold Wings rolled up and popped off. Imagine, one of them was a woman in her sixties. She had ridden her whole life and now here they were out for a spin — mother, father and forty-year-old son. She had one of the old Gold Wings that were hard to ride and I remember thinking, "Well, she is older, and she's riding, so you don't have to be young to do that." She handled that thing like it was a scooter. She was one of the very first women I saw on a bike.

I was in my late forties at that time and I thought, if this man has a heart attack, I won't be able to move this thing, so I should find out what he's doing with his hands and feet and stuff. I should learn how to ride, just as a safety precaution. I had no idea where brakes or the clutch or anything like that was.

My husband thought it was a wonderful idea. I took the written test and arrived at the course — me and nineteen young guys who were clearly comfortable on motorcycles. The only rule on the test was don't put your feet down; just keep going. The first thing I did, of course, was put my feet down, which meant I failed the test. I had never failed anything before in my life. I was devastated. I had to go home to my husband and my daughter, who was in university, and say I failed. I thought okay, the only thing I can do here is be a role model for my daughter and show her how to fail gracefully. I talked to her about that just last night and she said it never occurred to her that it was a failure.

I failed the first time, but I had the patience to pass eventually. Sometimes it takes a long time, and for those of us without testosterone, learning to ride sometimes takes a lot longer. I went back for the retest, worried sick. My sister-in-law, who's a physician, prescribed two pills of propranalol just to keep my nerves calm and I finally got my license.

Then I realized that there's no way on God's green earth that I was going to be able to move a Gold Wing. It was incredible that I even thought I might be able to do that. My husband encouraged me to start with something smaller, and we found a used, barely ridden Vulcan 500 that I rode for five thousand kilometers just around and around and around all the local, small roads that my husband took me on. The next year, I fell in love with an 1100 Virago and a few years ago, I bought myself a Gold Wing for my sixtieth birthday.

I had a death grip on the handlebars for my first ten thousand kilometers. You're not comfortable, but it does give you an incredible feeling of satisfaction. Not everybody can do it and I had done it. I got my license just after my fiftieth birthday, and it was all hooked into my brother as well. He had the kind of bike I originally wanted. He died when he was forty-eight and I was forty-nine. The whole early part of riding, I felt he was there with me. It was a way of me feeling closer to him.

When I first got my license and my little Vulcan, my husband and I tooted down to our Gold Wing club's Wednesday night at a local coffee shop. It was a lovely summer evening and everybody was outside. There must have been twenty or thirty other bikes out there, and of course all guys, because no other women rode at that time. The guys were all out there kicking the tires and telling lies. I rode into the parking lot and they all just stood there and clapped until I got off. I was close to tears. It wasn't just my husband who encouraged me. They were delighted that a woman was riding and offered all kinds of support. We had a young lad in the club at the time who turned sixteen and got his license, and they were just as encouraging with him.

I heard comments at my daughter's wedding. "I don't believe that Emily's mom rides the biggest bike I've ever seen." Stuff like that. Of course, people I work with just wouldn't expect a woman like me, who wears a suit at work and is a consultant, would be riding a bike, but I get more mileage out of that bike, because it's a source of conversation.

I seldom tell people I ride a bike. I just have a picture of my Gold Wing in my office, up on the wall. Most people never spot it, except for bikers. They walk in and they go, "Cool. Gold Wing."

The huge feeling of accomplishment drives us on to do it more and more and to improve our skills. I know it is risky, hard and uncomfortable. You might not succeed, but you might find it pays off in some other area. One of the wives in the club didn't take up motorcycling but she did take up playing the trombone. "If Hazel can learn to ride a motorcycle, then I can learn to play," she said.

Mary Barry

Occupation: program director, Frontier Team Building and
Summit Training
Location: St. Catharines, Ontario
Age: 43
Riding Discipline: street
Began Riding: 2004

Mary is my youngest sibling and I'm proud of her.

When she started riding, she had two young sons and her husband didn't ride. It's worked well for all of them. She likes to remind me of a time when she was six years old and my passenger on a ride through the ravine that bordered the farm. Apparently we had a spill and she burned her leg. She tells anyone who will listen that she was able to overcome that trauma and still get her license and help me with my business.

Mary found out in an unusual way that following our own instincts can have a curious effect. We can become leaders, and realize we actually have followers, while being oblivious to it happening. That can be another startling growth opportunity.

Growing up on the farm, we always had motorcycles around. The ones I really liked were the tiny little bikes with the fat tires that belonged to the neighbors. They would take me on those things, and you couldn't ride on the back because there was no back, so I rode on the tank with my feet up on the handlebars and my hands on the handlebars and probably no helmet. I always thought I would have a motorcycle, but as I got older, for some reason, it just went by the wayside.

In my late thirties, I had made some career changes and had some time. My sister was starting a motorcycle business and I was helping. I thought I should get some credibility, so I thought I would at least go and get my license. Right away, friends called and said that I could borrow their motorcycle to learn on, and they lent me this 450 Nighthawk for the whole summer. I was supposed to share it with one of their other friends but I think I got it more than he did.

I'd only had my license for a couple of days, but I think we went one thousand kilometers on that weekend. I was tired and scared most of the time because I wasn't used to it. After that, I felt pretty good on that bike. I rode as much as I possibly could that summer, trying to get my fix in.

When I picked up the Nighthawk, my friends cautioned me that something strange made people "Flock to the Hawk." They said, "You'll see."

Every Friday the 13th, motorcycles gather at Port Dover, a small fishing community on Lake Erie about an hour from my home. It attracts tens of thousands of bikers and on-lookers.

I got on the Nighthawk to ride to Port Dover, by myself. It was a horrible summer day, pouring, pouring rain. About twenty minutes into my ride, I pulled up to a stoplight, ready to make a left turn, and a guy, with a girl on the back, pulled up beside me. He was going straight and yelled to ask if I was going to Port Dover. When I nodded, he asked why I was turning left when he was going straight. I said, "Because I know a shortcut." He said, "Can I follow you?" "Sure."

So he is following me and I'm thinking, my God, people *do* Flock to the Hawk. I'm laughing about this. We're going past all these people who have pulled off to get out of the rain and we just kept riding and riding. At one section of the road, we saw a coffee shop and bakery and hundreds of bikes pulled over to get out of the weather. As soon as I passed it, there must have been a hundred bikes that pulled in behind me and they followed me all the way to Port Dover. Nobody was ahead of me and all I could see behind me in my rearview mirror were black skies, pouring rain and a hundred headlights. I don't even know what that feeling was, but it made me laugh. I thought, man, do they ever Flock to the Hawk. And that's how I learned to ride in the rain, with a crowd behind me and nervous about making a wrong turn.

At the end of the summer, when it was time to give the motorcycle back, I went to a local shop to purchase oil and a filter to do an oil change, and I came away with a motorcycle. It wasn't a new bike. I think it was fourteen years old. That's what I still ride and I've had it for five years now.

One thing I love about a motorcycle that's different from driving in a car, even with the windows down, is the smell of anything — good or bad. Like when you go past an orchard or you go past a farm or a vineyard. You can't smell it like that when you're in the car. And you can't feel the temperature change when you get close to the lake. It's a richer travel experience than in a car. You see things differently.

What's been reinforced through riding relates to some of the things we try and talk to our kids about. If there's something you want to do, you assess the risks, try to minimize the risk as much as you can and then go and do it and enjoy it.

People think you're going through a mid-life crisis when you're forty years old and you're starting to ride a bike. I've been accused of this on more than one occasion. I think when you *don't* do the things you want to do, *that's* when you're going to have a mid-life crisis.

One of the rewards I get, and it's hard to come by when you have young children at home, is solitude. I won't say quiet, because it's not quiet on the bike. But nobody's asking me for anything. Obviously it's one of the pleasures of parenthood and being in a family, but it's also sometimes overwhelming. So when I go out, it's just me. I like to have that alone time with my thoughts, or lack thereof, and that's one of the ways I get it.

Sometimes people question me because I've got two young boys and my husband doesn't ride. Obviously I've considered the risks and I try to make it as safe as I can, but I've got to live my life. I hope my kids do the same. At that point, you shouldn't worry about what might happen. It's a buzz kill; it takes the fun out of it. It will stop you from all of the rewards you can get, not just motorcycle riding, but from anything. You always face risks. You take risks and you get rewards.

CHAPTER 5

Dealing With the Unexpected

"You can sit back and let life go by or you can get on it."

—Activist Roxie Malone

THE WHOLE TOURISM BUSINESS was new to me and I ran into all kinds of start-up challenges in the first year that I hadn't expected — obtaining business and motorcycle insurance, incorporating my business, registering as a legal travel retailer, creating a compelling website and marketing. It was very different from the corporate world I'd left behind and a polar opposite to the nursing that marked the start of my professional life.

I had never been concerned with finances before, but I sure was now. I had to come to terms with getting to know myself and enjoying my own company. I wasn't really lonely, although I was alone much of the time. I had already learned feeling trapped in the wrong role can be the loneliest place there is.

My first motorcycle clients showed I was on the right business track. During our tours, people all discovered things inside themselves they didn't know were there, whether it was riding in the rain for the first time, traveling farther than they had ever gone or experiencing a part of the country they had never visited. Their smiles and jubilation were the best reward I could have asked for.

My birthday in May of 2004 fell on Mother's Day, as it had the day I came into the world. My seventy-eight-year-old mother wanted to go for a motorcycle ride, so we did. She held on to my waist tightly and her bony knees clamped against my hips for the first few miles, until she relaxed into the ride. When we got off, I remember laughing that, fifty years earlier, she had been trying to push me out, and now she was trying to hold on. We still continue the new tradition of that Mother's Day ride, although she needs a small step stool these days to get on and off. My sister has earned her license and for the past few years, she and her son have joined us on this very special ride.

The road spanning the summers of 2004 and 2005 was under construction when I went through. It had some smooth, scenic riding but lots of rough sections full of potholes, detours and abruptly changing conditions. It was treacherous at times and consequently a tremendous time of learning about myself. In addition to launching a new business, I started teaching and found that, even in colleges, students are tough on new instructors. I'm sure they could sense my insecurity and a few of them circled for the kill. I persevered, I learned and I succeeded.

Everything was new during this time: a new social circle, new relationships, new status as a single person, dating and no means of steady income. I had uprooted my whole life and now it was up to me to replant and rebuild according to a design I thought was best for who I was and what I wanted to do. Everything was, admittedly, a little topsy turvy.

Toward the end of the 2004 season, friends who had out-of-town motorcycling guests visiting for a day invited me to join them for a ride and barbecue. A few local riders were included, one of whom they were trying to set me up with. Cupid's arrow flew all right, but it hit an unintended person — someone from another country and in a whole different life. Hart and I were immediately attracted to each other, but I brushed it off because the timing was all off, among other things.

In 2005, a cast of dubious characters entered my life and it ended up being a pretty tumultuous year. I had it in my mind that I needed a business partner, for instance. I was still vulnerable and my self-confidence, faith and trust were not yet strong enough to keep me on my own course.

Problems came at me from all angles — business and personal relationships, financial and legal issues — all essentially from placing trust where it was ill deserved. I found myself lapsing into old, destructive behavior patterns, working sixteen-hour days, depleting my energy and losing any semblance of work/life balance. I thought I had left that kind of nonsense behind for good, but I learned the familiar is comfortable, even when it's not in one's best interest. I didn't recognize my own worth. Others did and wanted to exploit it.

Fortunately, I was blessed with a core group of loyal friends and family. With their support and compassion, I got through that stretch of road relatively unscathed and with my dignity intact. I am a strong believer in the adage that out of the darkest moments come the greatest light and growth, although it's hard when you're in it. It was merely a matter of picking myself up, dusting myself off and getting back on the metaphorical horse, in my case, an iron one. Those unsavory characters were actually gifts, although I didn't recognize them as such for quite a while. I considered my financial losses tuition for my Ph.D. in Life.

I was really enjoying my clients. It was increasingly fulfilling to watch their transformations as a result of our rides.

On one trip, I guided a group through some back country we knew would include a road with a small section of packed gravel. It was only about thirty feet, but if you've never been on gravel before, it can be scary. One of the women had just learned to ride and had a big, new cruiser, decked out with chrome, fringes everywhere and, wisely, engine guards. She had enjoyed being a passenger for years and had done a lot of touring with her husband. When he passed away unexpectedly, she decided to learn how to ride on her own.

I'm always counting the headlights of my group in my rear view mirror while I'm guiding, especially if the road has an obstacle. After I was through the gravel, I looked back and could see the new rider charging through, eyes wild and as big as saucers, hair and fringes all flying. But her eyes were focused on where she was going, her throttle was steady and at the right speed and she did just fine. She experienced another first and climbed another rung up the ladder of self-confidence.

The women whose stories are included in this chapter have come face to face with fear, in some cases that fear being their own mortality. By boldly staring down that fear and calling upon skills they've discovered through riding, they've become aware of even greater power extending far beyond themselves and their circles.

Sue Cannell

Occupation: executive assistant, Toronto Blue Jays Major League Baseball Club
Location: Toronto, Ontario
Age: 56
Riding Discipline: off-road street
Began: 1976

Don't ever tell Sue she can't do something. She won't listen anyway. Age forty is late to start trail riding, but her husband bought a dirt bike and she wasn't going to be left behind, even though this type of motorcycling can be extremely challenging physically and mentally.

She's used to winning in a man's world. Since 1977, she has been executive assistant to Paul Beeston, former president of Major League Baseball and now president of the Toronto Blue Jays.

I rode street, starting when I was about twenty-five. Then I had three kids, one right after the other, and I let it slide for many years. But my husband bought a dirt bike with all the equipment. I thought, well, the hell with this, I want one as well. I started riding off-road pretty late, at age forty, but I fell in love with the sport.

The first time out was at a gravel pit, a crazy spot with ATVs and motorcycles buzzing everywhere. There I was, a new rider with all my brand-new gear on — chest protector, elbow pads, boots. It was pretty intimidating. At that point I was frightened taking a little hill that was four feet high, but I persevered. I didn't know a whole lot of other riders and was always riding with my husband and his racing friend. It was frustrating because I was always left behind. Even though they would wait for me at the corners, I got to the point where I thought I might throw in the towel. Looking back now, I see it made me push more and become a better rider more quickly.

It's a release when you get out there and you're in the moment. You don't think of anything else. You're having so much fun and all your problems and everything go by the wayside. Rightly so, because you have to be a gazillion percent focused on what you're doing at that time.

My favorite ride was two days on the trail up in Algonquin, very intimidating for a newbie. One of the veteran riders led a group of beginners. He took his time and patiently got us through tough areas and around obstacles. I learned a lot from him, and that ride sold me on the sport I love. After all these years, I make an effort to take out novice riders, too.

Trail riding can be very dangerous and you have to keep your eyes always around the next corner. But I love the variety in trail riding and not knowing what's around the corner. It could be a stretch of water, a bunch of roots or a single track between trees, but it's always a challenge. I just kept going out to more and more trail rides, even though only a few gals were going. My skills kept getting better and I felt thoroughly fulfilled.

During one trail ride, I came to a difficult section I'd done before but I got pulled over by a guy who told me, "No, you can't do it." It was only because I was a woman that he pulled me off to the side and didn't want me to go up. I know people get stuck up in these areas. We have sweepers at the end of the ride who tow them or fix their bike to get them out. Well, I blasted out past him and I didn't have any problem whatsoever. That was a satisfying moment. Yes, I can do that, and don't label women riders in that way. Nobody ever tried again to stop me from going on any of the options.

Few women are in the sport and you really have to prove yourself before you get acceptance. Sometimes you can just sit back and take the easy route, but I always push myself into the options, because the more you put yourself through, the better rider you become.

My toughest race was the fiftieth anniversary Corduroy Enduro, which had about one hundred and eighty men and four women. The

race had a lot obstacles that were new to me, like deep-water cross-
ings, getting bogged down in mud and water. My bike kept conking
out in about two hundred kilometers of very rough terrain. Day two
was even harder. I had no strength left whatsoever. I had to sit down,
gather myself and get the courage up and the strength up to get my
bike out from where it was bogged down this time. I didn't finish
pretty by any means and but I did it! When I came back, though, I
had a total meltdown. It was so overwhelming I lost it and started
crying and shaking.

But there's nothing I back away from. Nothing really intimidates
me anymore. The type of riding I do at times is pretty extreme and
it's picked up my courage and my self-esteem.

The men don't intimidate me anymore, unlike the first two to
three years. Now I'm accepted, I'm one of the guys. I'm not really a
shy person, but it used to be hard to speak up with people I didn't
know, especially in crowds. But I joined the Ontario Federation of
Trail Riders and got elected to their board in my third year. I felt
good that they respected me enough to vote me in and I was with
them for five years, until it started affecting my job.

My husband and I have been involved with the Algonquin ride
for quite a few years now. Last year, we took it on ourselves with
some other volunteers and ended up with one hundred and seventy
riders, a record!

I'd like to encourage more females to enter the sport. I take my
time out on trail rides now and I take novice groups out and some
women do join in and quite enjoy it. Enduro racing is no piece of
cake but it's doable. It's a lot of fun and it's very satisfying.

My daughter is in the sport and she absolutely loves it. I look
forward to my grandchildren joining her.

Roxie Malone

Occupation: activist, former radio personality
Location: Edmonton, Alberta
Age: Top Secret
Riding Discipline: street
Began Riding: 1996

Roxie's strength is epic. Many lesser people would have given up had they gone through what she has, yet her indomitable spirit continues to shine. She says the word that best describes her is "determined."

Roxie would never walk, her mother was told three months after the baby was born. Roxie proved them wrong and uses the same strength now to deal with her daughter's health issues.

Roxie was a studio producer in Edmonton radio for fourteen years and the host of a couple of radio shows. Now she is a stay-at-home mom, her biggest and best role so far.

When she's not fighting for her daughter or her health, she's advocating for the rights of women, children and the handicapped. She personifies facing fear and knocking it out of the way. "Life is about going after what you want," she says. "It's not about sitting around and thinking and wishing and hoping, because it ain't gonna happen."

She never takes anything in life for granted and fully appreciates the power riding a motorcycle brings her.

I was born with spina bifida, a birth defect where the spine doesn't close properly. They cut the cyst off when I was three months old and when they did that, they cut all the nerve endings to the back of my legs, so I'm paralyzed from the waist down in the back of my legs. They told my mother I would never walk. But I can feel in the front of my legs and that's where all my power is.

Right from the beginning, when they told my mom I wouldn't walk, she said, "No, you are a doctor, not a fortune teller and she WILL walk." She instilled that in me at a very young age, that "you WILL walk," and it's because of her that I have all this strength and determination. Little did I know I'd need it later in life for my own daughter.

A boyfriend of ten years was a biker and when we broke up, I missed the lifestyle and decided to learn how to ride myself. I bought the bike and then I had to learn how to ride it. Because of my disability, I wasn't sure I'd be able to, but the worst case was that I'd have to turn it into a trike. I'm only five feet tall and have had to have a lot of custom work done so I can touch the ground.

I must have dropped that little Suzuki a million times during the course. The instructor said, "If you can't hold this little bike up, how are you going to hold that big Sportster up?"

Steely determination made me the only one in the class with a perfect score. He said, "You'll be talked about for years, because I get all these able-bodied people in here who tell me they can't do it, and if anybody shouldn't have been able to do it, it should have been you."

It was almost overwhelming the second day, though. I couldn't grasp the clutch concept, but after a while it was just like breathing. I understand why able-bodied people would give up, because they don't have the courage and the drive and they don't want it that bad. I wanted it real bad.

I like to run into people who say they can't do it. Here you are, an able-bodied person, and you don't have the faith in yourself to be able to do it. I've sort of turned that around for a lot of people because they look at me and they say, "Well, how stupid do I feel now?" That often gives me a sense of power, when I help other people find their sense of power.

I've always been fiercely independent, so it was a given that riding was a lifestyle I would choose. It has also made me closer to the community. Within the biker community, everybody knows everybody else. It's just one big family and that's a good feeling, to be a part of that. My attitude has changed, too. I'm a little cockier because I'm *proud* I've done this. Against all odds, I've not taken no for an answer.

The third year I got my bike, we went off to a large rally, and I actually won the show 'n shine. It was one of my most memorable experiences, other than getting married on a bike. Out of three thousand bikes, he put the trophy down in front of me. Now I have a whole wall full of show 'n shine trophies.

When I was pregnant with my daughter, my doctor told me not to ride. It was too dangerous and I was carrying something very precious. It was tempting when all my friends went out, but I was able to put that thought aside. One day it was so nice out that we were tempted to take out the bikes, but didn't. That very day, I started to bleed and ended up in the hospital on two solid weeks of bed rest, trying to get the pregnancy to twenty-five weeks. At twenty-five weeks and three hours — out she came, all one pound seven ounces of her.

You clear your head when you're riding. That's the best stress therapy there is. It really helped me with the challenge of having her in the hospital for five months.

Taking on the federal government to advocate for maternity benefits[7] was something concrete I could fight for. I wasn't fighting for myself. I was fighting so the next people who come up behind me aren't going to run into the same situation. I realize not all parents are in a position to take something like this on. I didn't get the legislation passed in time for me to benefit from it, but I definitely put a ripple in the water.

The first five months of our daughter's life were an ordeal and what she's been through has been sheer hell since then. She needed throat surgery to expand her constricted airway, which meant keeping her in a medically induced coma for eight days to let her throat

---

[7]   In May 2007, Roxy Malone and over 1,000 petitioners urged changes in employment insurance to provide additional maternity benefits for complications due to pregnancy. They won.

heal. Weaning her off the morphine with methadone took another month and a half, and the withdrawal was worse than the surgery. The surgery wasn't even successful. Now she has a tracheotomy, and will for two years. But for the first time in her life, she can really breathe.

She has accepted all of this way better than her mom and dad have.

My left foot used to be my good one, and it could hold my bike up quite nicely and I could shift with it and everything. Then I began to experience problems. The neurosurgeons say they will not perform back surgery on me because the risks outweigh the benefits, and I will probably never move my left foot again. I am wearing orthotic braces now that make walking a lot easier.

As soon as all this is settled down with our daughter, I'll have to get a handlebar clutch put on my bike. I'm not ready to hang up my helmet and get out of the front seat just yet. If I have to, well, I got twelve years I wasn't expecting in the first place. Everything's a bonus. Walking's a bonus. If I was not able to walk tomorrow, well, I got a lot of years I was never supposed to get. It all depends how you look at life.

Maybe that's the reason for everything that has happened to me, that I'm supposed to be a role model and inspire other people.

Kate Insley

Occupation: co-owner Barrie Harley-Davidson
Location: Barrie, Ontario
Age: 52
Riding Discipline: street
Began Riding: 1996
Website: barriehd.com

Cancer was no match for Kate Insley. In 1991, at age thirty-five, with two young children, she was diagnosed with sarcoma in her leg muscles. At the time, her motorcyclist husband had just ordered his first Harley-Davidson and she was a reluctant passenger at first. The right Harley Owners Group, however, opened up a different world that included new friends who supported her through her diagnosis, treatment and recurrences.

She fell in love with motorcycling and got her own license. Her husband bought a Harley-Davidson dealership and she joined him there.

Motorcycling changed her life, with cancer as the underlying catalyst, she says. After a long, hard fight, she's cancer-free.

I met a man who had a motorcycle. We went through the whole thing about getting married, no money, kids, no money. In 1991 he decided to get his first Harley–Davidson. About a month after he ordered his bike, I found out I had cancer. He said he would cancel the bike, but I said no, this is something you want.

We got the motorcycle and I'd spend time on it, but it wasn't really fun. Then we hooked up with a very small, close-knit Harley Owners Group (HOG), and the ladies became almost like a support group.

I'm a control freak and I'd had my life planned out. When something like cancer happens to you, you realize you're not in control of your life. You take a step back and look at what's happening. I was thirty-five years old, I had two young kids and I felt perfectly fine. But I had sarcoma in my leg muscles. Terry Fox had it in his bones.

My cancer returned in 1993 and traveled into my lungs. I went through four courses of chemo, two surgeries and then more chemo — and got all the bald jokes I wanted to hear. The whole HOG chapter came just to be there for me and to remind me about the big world out there, rather than the hospital I was in.

I remember climbing on the back of the bike to go to Milwaukee, having lost all my hair yet again with chemo, and I was amazed to see everyone there wearing bandanas. I fit right in and didn't look sick. When we returned, it was time for my fourth and final treatment. I climbed on the motorcycle the very next day — my oncologist probably freaked — and hung out with my friends and family that weekend. One of the things they teach you is to learn to laugh. The endorphins you get are supposed to make you feel better, and trust me, it works. With the laughing and the carrying on, everything seemed fine.

In November of 1994, my oncologist found two more tiny spots of cancer. They operated, and I've been clean to this day.

In the course of all that, I fell in love with the motorcycle, because on the back of the bike, I wasn't sick. I was just a rider and I had this whole group of friends who *all wore bandanas*. It was just one of those warm things, a warm friendly, family group thing.

In 1995, my husband went to work as a service manager for a Harley-Davidson retailer. Two years after that, he and a group of others had an opportunity to buy the dealership. With much soul searching and a very supportive banker, we made the leap. Gradually since then, I've bought the shares up from the others and now it's just my husband and I. Three years ago, I left a senior management position at the municipality where I'd been working for thirty-one years. People ask me how I made the change. It was not in my game plan, but cancer never is either. I'm here, I'm surviving, I'm fifty-two years old and I just get on my bike and I'm twenty years old again.

One day back in 1996, we were traveling and I kept thinking, I'm a very independent person, and I'm in a very dependent position on the back of the motorcycle. I'd gone several years beyond the cancer-free date, and you start to build up some confidence that you have a future. I finally said to myself, if something ever happened to Bruce while we were traveling, I wouldn't know what to do with this thing. So, I took it upon myself to get my license. I had a little 250 Honda for the summer, but I had trouble keeping up with my husband on his big Ultra. On Labor Day, I climbed onto my own Sportster. I'm now on my third Harley, a Heritage.

Motorcycling has had a huge impact on my life. I don't know if the leap would have been so dramatic without the cancer. Having said that, though, I am a tomboy, I am independent, I have earned my own wage since I was eighteen years old, and I love that sense of freedom and no worries out on the road.

I've worked all my life in a man's world. I started out in the engineering section as a clerk in the road department and followed a natural progression to senior manager. I speak my mind and as long as everybody respects what's going on, we're all stronger for it.

When I see other women riders, I realize they're exploring freedom and independence. I could never understand women who stayed at home, and had to depend on their husbands for money, and their social circle was in the neighborhood because they didn't have a car. I look at the riders and I say, good for you, girls. I think it gives you a very good feeling inside, makes you a stronger person and better able to deal with critical issues, like cancer, family, divorce.

I've had guys come over the center line at me. I've locked up my back tire. If you've got the proper training and the confidence, though, you know how to react. Sometimes riders say, but it all happens in a split second. I understand that, but nothing is more frightening than cancer. I'm thinking about the day I stood there and they told me I had cancer. I had a five year old and a seven year old. Describe frightening. I get concerned, I get upset riding in the dark and the rain. Nobody likes to do that on strange roads, but it's all relative to the road you're on and your confidence in yourself.

If I'm riding on a beautiful road that happens to stop and turn to loose gravel, I get upset. But I can't turn around and go back. I've got to persevere and go forward.

I have dropped my bike three times, all at slow speeds. Once it wasn't even running. You know what? You get up, you dust yourself off and away you go. You suffer through the embarrassment if someone happened to see you do it and you say, oh well, it could have been worse.

A lot of women out there want to get into motorcycling, but they're not sure about it, or their mates aren't supportive or their mates are putting them down. If you feel you can do it, try it. Some women aren't meant to do it. But if you are able to get out riding, make your ride your own. Don't let *anybody* tell you what you can or can't do within the law of your motorcycle.

Elizabeth Bokfi

Occupation: freelance writer, snapshot dreamer and
wanna-be rockstar
Location: Orillia, Ontario
Age: 43
Riding Discipline: street
Began Riding: 1982
Website: ReverbNation.com/OvertymeMusic

I sought out Liz's website a few years ago after reading her articles in trade magazines. I was intrigued by this Road Gypsy with the tenacious spirit. To start with, I was impressed that at five feet tall, she was able to manage a fully loaded Harley, sometimes with a passenger, and tour across the country.

That paled in comparison with the candid, poignant account of her experience after the discovery of a tumor in her left ankle, resulting in a below-the-knee amputation. Her '97 Harley-Davidson Super Glide has been outfitted with a sidecar and her dream is a return ride to Alaska.

She describes learning to "live" again as the toughest job of her life and says motorcycling was key. She now devotes time not only to motorcycle-related causes, but also to encouraging other amputees toward recovery.

I've always been interested in motorcycles, and as a child I had a friend who would take me across the railway tracks on the back of his dirt bike. Dad agreed that when I turned sixteen, I could buy a bike out of my college fund. That turned out to be a 185 cc '79 Honda Twinstar. Around the same time, Mom entered a contest and won a Beluga Yamaha scooter. She and my dad learned to ride it and we all ended up going to take our bike licenses at the same time. That was really cool. It just snowballed from there. I got a bigger bike and started touring very early on.

On my first trip, a friend and I got on our bikes with a pocket full of money and rode from Orillia to Grand Falls, New Brunswick, approximately twelve hundred kilometers, all in one shot. I had ridden with makeup on and you learn very quickly not to. We rode side by side for three hours with our turn signals flashing because we were afraid of getting run over by a transport truck in thick fog.

By the time we got to Grand Falls, it was four-thirty a.m. There were no vacancies but the guy behind the counter let us sleep in the upstairs hallway on sofas until the first people left. He woke us up at six-thirty, we moved to a vacated room and he didn't even charge us for staying the night. He said, "No, I've been there. I've ridden."

My favorite, most challenging and most rewarding trip was the one to Alaska I took with a friend in 2003. We left on our big Harleys in early June because my goal was to be at the dome in Dawson City to join the celebration for the summer solstice. We had about four days of sunny weather for the five weeks we were gone. The rest was torrential rain, gale-force winds that peeled roofs off, slush, ice and snow. It was crazy. Luckily, I had purchased a plug-in vest and gloves for this trip.

At one point near Haines Junction, the road was under construction and we were riding through rocks, potholes, gravel and clay, so it was very greasy. I was riding my clutch in heavy traffic, trying to keep my distance so I could keep it rolling, because I was on the balls of my feet with this huge load on and I knew that if I had to put my feet out I was toast. But I didn't dump my bike once. Not once.

After the discovery of a tumor in my left ankle, I underwent a below-the-knee amputation on January 26, 2007. The rehabilitation, combined with the chemotherapy, has proven to be the toughest job I have ever had to work at in my life.

Once I went into the rehabilitation center, I was shocked it wasn't just a matter of strapping the prosthetic device on and being able to walk. I was discouraged with my endurance and didn't realize the gravity of the situation. When I realized I wasn't going to walk for a few months, I got scared I wouldn't be riding that season. I immediately started preparations to put a sidecar on and started thinking about ways I could ride. I told myself, "I'm going to ride with or without the leg."

My initial thought was to take a piece of wood and strap it to my residual limb and shift like that. And then I thought, no, I can put the shifter on the right side, so I did that. I felt a lot better after I was riding again. I thought, okay, I'm not walking yet, but I'm riding. It gave me the strength, gumption and willpower to see myself walking again.

That was a bad time for me. I was depressed. I was in a wheelchair for seven months. I was used to going one hundred miles an hour in my daily life and all of a sudden I came to a grinding halt, so I was really closed in. Riding gave me freedom.

For a time, I had a hard time seeing into the future. Normally, you plan a week from now, maybe you plan a month from now, or in May you're going to do this. I had real difficulty with that. Once I started riding again, though, I started planning little day trips, so it got me over that hump.

Shortly after my chemo and not long after I had the prosthetic, I ventured out on a three hundred and twenty-five kilometer trip to Maine, peanuts if you're able-bodied and well. I wasn't even walking and was bald as a cue ball. I was hauling this sidecar and it was very strenuous work. I had to stop every fifteen minutes because I was in so much pain with my back. I kept saying, I can't make it home, I can't make it home. But I did. I rode the last ten kilometers on gravel and through bear country with a flat tire on my sidecar. I don't know if I could do it today.

Some people tell me I'm brave. I don't see myself that way. Sometimes I look back at what I've done and wonder what I was thinking. The truth is, you don't think about it. You go ahead and do it. If you stop and think about it too long, you'll talk yourself out of it.

The whole riding experience draws me — the backpacking, the air and the smells, particularly clover. People come up and talk to you. You're sitting up higher on a bike so you have a different physical viewpoint.

Riding is always such an exhilarating thing. When I start talking about my travels with my boyfriend, he's mesmerized. "When you talk, I see your eyes and I see you're back there again." When I'm heading out of Calgary toward the Rockies, I still get that rush. Or heading to Denver and I see the Rockies in front of me, there's just nothing like that. I get goose bumps. I start crying. I get emotional. That is the moment when I know I'm in the right place.

I write a lot of my songs on the road and incorporate my experiences into them. That lets me relive them every time someone wants me to tell my story.

I know I have driven my parents crazy. They have only me and one granddaughter. When I took my daughter out to Newfoundland on the bike a few years ago, I thought they were going to lose it. But I would say, "Well, Mom, why be ordinary when you can be extraordinary?"

I still want to go to the Northwest Territories next year. My parents say, "Couldn't you try something a little closer?" They do understand, though, that I don't want to wait until I'm sixty-five. People get sick when they're sixty-five. I want to do this now. They understood this when I got sick. "You know, it seems like you were preparing for this all along. I see now why you want to do this."

Catherine Swift

Occupation: president and chief executive officer, Canadian Federation of Independent Business; director, C.D. Howe Institute; past president, Empire Club
Location: Toronto, Ontario
Age: 54
Riding Discipline: street
Began Riding: Mid 1970s

I remember Catherine as a senior economist with the Toronto Dominion Bank, often sought out by the media for interviews then and now because of her expertise. I had no idea she was a biker! I also had no idea she later used her motorcycle to help conquer illness. Given her drive, her cancer probably didn't stand much of a chance to start with.

Catherine joined the Canadian Federation of Independent Business in 1987. One reason she enjoys working with entrepreneurs is because of their self-sufficiency and independence, qualities she admires.

She's a dedicated volunteer as well.

I started riding in my early twenties. I found it very liberating. I've always been independent and into trying new or different things. For quite a while, children, a demanding career and volunteer work have been my priorities and most of my riding has been as a passenger. When my life frees up in the next few years, I intend to get back into it.

A certain amount of everybody's propensity to cultivate their power is hard-wired and it came naturally to me. In my younger days, I was always in the student parliament, heading up something or captaining a sports team. I gravitated to risky sports, mainly competitive gymnastics, where you can really get yourself into some pickles. I injured myself a fair bit and always managed to get back on the horse. It's a bit of risk-taking, but a calculated risk, not a stupid risk.

Growing up, I was very close to my dad. Sadly, he passed away when I was young and it was a huge blow. He was always a big volunteer person. I do a variety of different things, whether it's helping out people who are down on their power and less able to do things themselves, or igniting youth entrepreneurs. I've been president of the Empire Club, which brings in interesting speakers from all over the world, and I'm still on their board. I'm also on the board for the C.D. Howe Institute (a leading Canadian nonpartisan public policy think tank) because that's research and my first love.

Motorcycling reinforces your own ability to be independent, to do your own thing and not to rely on other people. It's another skill set to be very in tune with your body and the machine, like the sports I've done. It's a physical awareness as well as knowing where your mind is at any given time. Obviously, the two are working in sync ideally.

Entrepreneurs, like motorcyclists, are dynamic and deal with risk all the time. They're going to take a flyer and they're going to have confidence in themselves to achieve their dreams. I've been in this small-business realm for a long time, so obviously it suits me very well.

I'm a very optimistic person, but it's calculated. I believe you make your own weather. If you are optimistic, it's a lot more likely that good things will happen. I've read a lot of material over the years on leadership, and people aren't going to want to follow a given leader if they're negative.

I see people who mope around and I wonder if they're enjoying being miserable. I don't get it. If you've got the choice of being up or down, why not be up?

During one trip to Cape Breton, I was stung by a wasp. I'll never forget that experience or the gorgeous day it happened. It got under my T-shirt and stung me several times. It was such a sharp pain, like somebody stabbed me. Here we were in a scenic area on a beautiful day and then, all of a sudden, whamo! In cases like that, I go immediately to my quiet place and literally will myself to be calm. You stop, you deal with it, but you just continue on, just like with most of life's startling moments.

A few years ago, I found a lump in my breast that turned out to be cancer. It was relatively small and easily dealt with. People used to say I was lucky, and I'd say, "Actually, lucky is *not* having cancer." But that being said, you deal with it. The worst part of it was the damn chemo and that you feel sick all the time. I tried to distract myself in whatever way I could, and one of them was riding. I can zone out somewhat on everyday things, and it helps to get me out of my head and not brood on tough stuff happening in life.

Whether it's riding or anything else, you have to believe you have an impact, or why would you do it? With the business I'm in now, we have to believe we make a difference and we *know* we make a difference. If you don't try to make things better, then you're guaranteed not to. Make a run at it and it doesn't mean you're going to succeed all the time, but, boy, if you never try, you're darn sure you're never going to experience success.

Motorcycling is still viewed as a rebellious thing, not just for women, but in general. It affirms independence and our capability to do something different. It's even more atypical for a woman, as it's not a particularly girly thing to do

My favorite form of exercise is running on trails in a nice open area. I've always been a big fan of camping and being out in nature and there are similar elements with riding. You're not sealed off from things. About three years ago, I was able to buy a cottage in an area with beautiful roads and lovely rolling hills, and everything's just so stunning. My dream is to ride around my cottage. That's a heavenly combination of things, to my way of thinking.

CHAPTER 6

Connecting With Spirit

"This is the moment you know you're in the right place."

—Writer Elizabeth Bokfi

SOMEWHERE AROUND THIS TIME, I realized I'd had all the power I needed all along. Just like on the motorcycle, I controlled how much power was being used. I didn't have to look to others for it. In fact, they couldn't give me power, although some would gladly take it. I had always trusted people to do the right thing and act honorably. Realizing not everyone shared my code was painful at the time, but it strengthened me.

I had established that my personal and professional mission was to facilitate the creation of an environment in which others could push through their own barriers, discover their own power and thrive. One can create such an environment in many ways. My contribution was to do it through motorcycling.

Now three years into it, I felt I had to reassess my game plan, going back to my original drawings and focusing on the priorities I had established. I can never minimize the role of, nor my gratitude for, the wonderful people who appeared in my life during this time of rapid change. Genuine help would materialize from nowhere. One of the difficulties with focusing on service is in being able to draw the distinction between serving your purpose and giving away energy. Often difficult choices needed to be made. Advice gurus and networking and marketing experts were all attracted by a novel idea. After a certain amount of trial and error, however, I accepted that none of them knew what was right for me and my business better than my own inner guidance system.

Always, the fear of how I would make it financially gnawed at my stamina. Motorcycle riding in my area can be only a seasonal business. I consoled myself that I would always have human resources consulting to fall back on, but I ended up directing significant resources to going after something I didn't even like any more.

Sometimes we're so caught up in the day to day we forget to take stock and recognize how far we've progressed and reward ourselves. But when I started my cross-country jaunt, I focused on one day at a time. Every day I would get up and go riding, heading west and covering new ground. Each day was easily manageable and enjoyable, full of new experiences and people. Before I knew it, I was at the Pacific Ocean and turned south. Progress was easy to measure.

Giving challenges too much stage time can camouflage success. At the end of 2006, I resurrected my coaching notes and listed my successes of the previous year. I surprised myself. I had accomplished some pretty neat things and if I continued to focus and apply myself in the right direction, it would all work out. Just like the stream following its nature, I needed to stop resisting the flow. It was wearing me out. I had thought I was beyond that, but vestiges of old behavior patterns were still lurking in the shadows.

Next, I evaluated my priorities against my activities to identify those that weren't aligned with my vision, that were depleting my energy without accomplishing what I really wanted to do. There was only one thing to do: close some doors behind me and keep moving forward, eyes looking where I wanted to go — the same thing you're taught when you learn to ride.

One of my hardest lessons was that matter of learning to follow my own internal guidance. I really didn't care what others thought of me, but I was under the mistaken impression that they knew more about what was best for me than I did.

If I was creating an environment for others to push their limits and thrive, I had to be a role model. Several years earlier, the Motorcyclists Confederation of Canada (MCC) had been formed by a group of dedicated enthusiasts with the prompting and support of the motorcycle industry. The national advocacy organization would promote and protect the rights of motorcyclists in Canada. In 2006, the founding members were ready to hold their first elections for the board of directors.

Giving back to my community was another of my personal musts and serving with MCC looked like a perfect way. Even considering taking this on would never have happened in my previous life. I ran for the position to represent Ontario and to my surprise was elected.

It was not the first MCC in my life. In 1920, in the former Soviet Union, the Mennonite Central Committee was established to offer a bowl of soup and a slice of bread to starving villagers — like my grandparents. The group remains active around the world, offering help to those who need it, regardless of race, religion or political orientation. How fitting that I was elected to another MCC. I'm proud to carry on a tradition of serving my community.

The personal relationship I wished for remained elusive. Most of the time, I was quite happy on my own with a small circle of close friends nearby and Hart as my mostly virtual confidante. In spite of the distance, the fates would conspire to bring us together every so often and send signs of encouragement, just when it was most needed, often against all odds. One year we arranged time off and planned a motorcycling vacation in the south. A terrible snowstorm descended on the Toronto airport the day I was to depart. Most flights were cancelled, yet mine, although delayed, got me to my destination. Another time, we sent each other the exact same Christmas card, something that made even our hard-bitten biker friends shiver.

Friends who saw us together claimed we must have been together in another lifetime and our souls had found each other again in this one. We had a natural ease with each other and we felt at home when we were together, but we faced significant challenges. We both knew it, struggled with it and considered our relationship a precious gift. One thing I was certain of: time together, whether it was virtual or real time, always nourished my soul and gave me a new awareness of who I was and inspired me to proceed with renewed vigor.

The stories in this chapter all come from women who have discovered the restorative power of nourishing their souls through riding. By quieting their minds and allowing this experience, they've been able to arrive at profound insights on personal challenges.

Laura Culic

Occupation: visual artist; chief motorcycle instructor
Location: Toronto, Ontario
Age: 47
Riding Discipline: street
Began Riding: 1982
Website: lauraculic.com

Laura portrays the ever-changing effects of light on landscape in her fine art. Being alone with her thoughts and reveling in the insights of the present moment, whether through art, yoga or riding, gives her a high.

Her art captures a particular moment in time and makes that moment indelible, while everything around it changes. It is stillness and transformation, something she likens to riding. The awareness that has come from riding has given her the courage to take on tasks she would never have considered otherwise.

I was in my twenties and a full-time student at the Ontario College of Art (OCA) when I went for my first ride as a passenger. I've always been an independent sort of person and realized right away that I could do this by myself, even though I didn't have a car license. A car just seemed like so much to learn. But here was this tiny thing. You can go fast, and you can control it all by yourself.

My boyfriend — my parents didn't like him — helped me choose a bike and stored it at his place so they wouldn't find out. When the insurance company mailed the policy to my home, the jig was up. My parents gave me an ultimatum. I could sell my motorcycle and continue to live with them and they'd help me with my tuition, or I could keep my motorcycle and move out. I love my parents but it wasn't a difficult decision to go and live with my boyfriend at his mom's house. I used to commute to OCA on my bike with my portfolio over my shoulder. My parents still don't want to hear about me riding or see it. It's only been twenty-seven years, so maybe they'll still come around.

It made me really proud when I first started riding that I was able to ride difficult roads and keep up with the boys. It was really rare for girls to be doing that in the early eighties. I wasn't doing it because of the shock value of being a girl in a guy's world, but that definitely made me feel unique.

Yoga, painting and motorcycling are similar for me in that I'm alone. They all require one hundred percent commitment and concentration and give me the same high. I don't start wondering where we are going to sleep tonight, what we are going to have for dinner, what's on my grocery list. Nothing. I am in That Moment. When it's going well, I don't have room for any other thoughts, good or bad. When I stop riding, it's like after I finish yoga. It's like I've been away and am renewed and refreshed.

I love painting landscapes of places I'm familiar with and capturing a particular moment. I'm probably most fascinated by changing seasons or changing times, like times of day, say early morning with the mist just lifting. It's moving; it's not just a summer scene. I'm making a statement that's not changing but the place is changing, or the place is staying the same and I'm changing. It's an overriding sensation when I look at the landscape.

I'm aware of smells, temperature changes, the feel of the air and sensations like that, and that's partly why motorcycling is so cool. It's part of riding and part of what I'm thinking about when I'm painting, too. They connect that way.

I was always shy and reserved, but when I took the motorcycle course, I realized I wanted to be an instructor. After I'd been riding for eight or nine years, I decided it was time. I'd separated from my partner and wanted to do something empowering. I called the college where I had taken lessons and the timing was fortuitous; they hadn't trained new instructors for seven years and were taking applications.

It was brutal. I had to stand up in front of all the other candidates and practice teaching lessons. Speeches in high school had been torture, torment. So practicing teaching was really hard. But I was a rider and good at it. That gave me confidence. Still, it took a couple of years of teaching before I was not a nervous wreck on my way in.

A lot of times, you can easily spot newer riders. They're not as skilled and I feel almost embarrassed for them. It takes time for them. When I see an excellent woman rider, it's superb. The way they sit on a bike is a thing of beauty.

The whole motorcycle industry has traditionally been a boy's club, so becoming a chief instructor was a huge accomplishment for me. When the three senior chiefs invited me to become a chief, I felt as though I'd really made it. Last year, the pièce de résistance was when Madeleine (her story is in Chapter Two) and I designed and developed a program and got approval for our college to offer a senior course.

I have a really good sense of my contribution in our instructor group because I am in a position of power, yet I feel as though most of the other instructors still find me approachable and they'll come to me as the person who's going to have the most empathy and understanding about their problems as an instructor.

Being able to impart all this knowledge to other people is empowering. The fact that I can guide how this experience is going to unravel for them is pretty empowering. What I tell them is going to shape them as riders, develop their thinking processes beyond riding and keep them safe.

Kersty Franklin

Occupation: psychotherapist, clinical sexologist, holder of doctorate in human sexuality, bed and breakfast owner
Location: Orangeville, Ontario
Age: 54
Riding Discipline: street
Began: 1976
Websites: drkersty.com, streambb.com

I needed a place to stay in December, 2002, while I waited for my apartment to be ready, and I ended up at The Stream, operated by Kersty and her husband, John. They were both fascinating: she a psychotherapist and he a geological engineer. The Stream, with its wooded setting, three small waterfalls and outdoor Jacuzzi, all under a blanket of snow, was the perfect place to stay for the first two nights of my new life.

Years later, I learned she had once ridden a motorcycle. As I was researching for this book, she happened to answer an email from me that she found from four and a half years previously. Clearly, her story had to be told.

In contrast with most of the other women in this book, Kersty does not own her own bike and hasn't ridden for many years. Two jobs and caring for her husband, who has Parkinson's disease, leave little time. Interestingly, she lives on one of the most popular motorcycling roads in Ontario.

Motorcycles have entered her life at strategic times, when she has needed an illuminating boost to remind her of her own power. She knows one will be there for her again if it's needed.

I grew up in Florida and was riding a motorcycle at sixteen, before I even had my driver's license. I had a friend with a 360 Honda who taught me how to ride on the back roads. Within about three weeks, I felt I knew everything there was to know. Then my buddy lent me his bike to show my parents I could ride. On the way home, via the back roads, I hit a tree root and flew through the trees. Miraculously, I was barely scathed, but the bike was in bad, bad shape, so I couldn't get it home. My parents forbade me to get my motorcycle license for years.

Eventually, I found out that if you went to renew your driver's license and you told them you had a motorcycle license, they just put it on your license without checking. So that's what I did. I went home, showed my mom and dad I had my license and went out and bought my first motorcycle, a 185 Moto Guzzi, a little racing bike, and I loved it.

Then I joined the United States Army and put my bike riding on hold for a while.

Basic training was very tough. I weighed about one hundred and fifty-six pounds, but the Army said I should weigh one hundred and forty-eight. Those of us who were overweight had to sit at a table with a sign saying "Fat WACs." (WAC stands for Women's Army Corps.)

My drill sergeant hated me. She used to make me run with my arms across my breasts because she didn't want anyone to see my jiggling breasts. For eight weeks I was put down and by the end it almost felt like torture.

The highlight of my basic training was meeting a drill sergeant from another platoon. I was doing a project and somehow the talk turned to motorcycles and he said, "If you want, when you get your weekend off, I've got an old bike in the back sitting around that you could borrow."

He gave me the bike for a whole weekend! I just felt as though I found myself again on that weekend, riding through fabulous country on the back roads around Anniston, Alabama.

I had felt as though I was in a concentration camp. Getting that bike that weekend and being free again was the antidote. I went to a state park and just sat there, looking at the water with that feeling of total freedom.

Every human being should know how to ride a motorcycle, because of those feelings of freedom.

I have done many things to empower and enrich myself many times over since then, but that was the very first time I felt on top of the world despite all the adversity in my life at that time.

I attended the University of Akron and got my undergraduate degree in psychology. My whole income from the military was a very small monthly stipend and full tuition for university. Otherwise, I was a really poor full-time student working part-time for the National Park Service and I didn't have money to maintain or own a bike. I probably didn't ride again until I was studying for my master's degree and rode for a while with friends who always lent me one.

The time when I was taking my master's program was a really grueling one for me, as I was also overcoming many personal struggles. I had already been divorced and I felt as though my life was a failure. But every time I got on a bike I felt whole again.

It was bizarre that I was always able to find a motorcycle when I needed it, and that played out all the way until I was in my middle thirties. By then I had moved to Gainesville in Florida. I still didn't own a bike. I'd borrow one every now and then or rent one. Drivers in Florida are horrible, though, so I decided to give up riding there. Then I moved to Ontario, and in eleven years I think I've probably ridden only twice.

I would certainly never ever turn down a ride, because I still love it. There's nothing quite like the exhilaration of being on a bike. I don't even know how to explain it, because it's so different even from riding in a convertible. Riding really can help you to hone your listening to your instincts. I know I had times I trusted my instincts with a bike and things went better. It also helped me regain my sense of personal power.

I grew up with some pretty bizarre dramatic events. About the time I was seventeen, I started realizing the universe would give me everything I need, and it always has. But my husband is getting so ill and I worry now the universe is not going to help me stay with the man I would like to be with for the rest of forever.

I'm glad to see a woman writing a book about women who ride motorcycles. It makes me want to ride again.

Meg Thorburn

Occupation: epidemiologist
Location: Guelph, Ontario
Age: 54
Riding Discipline: off-road, dual-sport, street
Began: 1994

Meg avows that even when things are unbelievably bad, if she's on a bike, everything is good. And she has first-hand knowledge of what unbelievably bad is.

Two weeks after undergoing what she thought was a routine hysterectomy, she was diagnosed with a rare uterine sarcoma. For the next three months, whenever the weather permitted, she traveled to appointments by motorcycle. She rode quickly, picturing herself outracing the cancer cells. She maintains her motorcycle saved her life spirit.

When the cancer returned, she was given a five percent chance of survival and had some serious decisions to make. She chose to live.

A group of trail-riding friends established Meg's Ride, an annual trail ride for women that raises funds for local cancer-treatment facilities. Meg has attended them all, except for the one when she was off crossing the Continental Divide by motorcycle.

Even before her diagnosis, she was astounding and inspiring others with her skill and tenacity. She won her first National Enduro in 2001 at age forty-seven.

Her degree of enlightenment and the strength she has been able to draw on through meditating, bicycling and riding is phenomenal, and stronger than the disease that visited her.

I've always been a real outdoors person and environmentally conscious, and probably my main shtick was road bicycling. Living in

California, I could ride year-round so I would put ten thousand miles a year on my road bicycle. When I discovered mountain biking, that added even more miles. Then I met my partner, who was a dirt biker, and I fell in love. But at first I had this very dichotomous black/white idea — dirt biking is bad. I really liked him and he seemed like a very well-rounded, tree-hugging kind of guy, yet he was a dirt biker.

Our separate paths led us to Ontario, where we were both involved as volunteers for music festivals in a major way. One weekend, he invited me out for a trail ride to some nice ones he'd found, with berry patches and so on. I went on the back of his bike through all this single-track trail, which is the kind of stuff I love to trail run or ride on my mountain bike. I thought, "This is fun! I've got to get one of these!" Just like that I was transformed.

He desperately tried to talk me out of it, because I was thirty-nine or forty — old to be learning trail riding, because you fall a lot. I held off, but fortunately I had a good friend, a fellow professor who was retiring from racing dirt bikes, and he helped me buy a bike when my partner was away.

A lot of things in my life have come very easily for me. Dirt biking did not at all. I'm a very clumsy person; I don't have good balance or coordination. To have something you're just so naturally bad at and decide you're going to get good at it — that was part of why I embraced dirt biking as quickly as I did. I was going to figure it out and not let it defeat me.

My sabbatical was coming up and I'd arranged to work in Honduras. I was going to be working with really poor farmers and needing to be out in the field a lot. My partner decided he would take the year off because he was doing contracts at that time and could easily arrange it into his schedule. We decided we would trailer the bikes to the Mexican border and then ride down to Honduras. That gave me six months to become a good enough dirt-bike rider for what turned out to be a trip of nineteen thousand kilometers, mostly off-pavement.

This was something we really embraced together. I got to be a much better rider and we did a second trip to Central America. I got really comfortable on the bigger dirt bikes as well as my smaller race bike.

In 2000 Suzuki decided to put together an off-road national team, and I've been a national enduro champion four times now. Several women were substantially faster than I was, but I committed to going to every race. Although I got injured a lot, I usually made it through the season. It was more my persistence than my speed that got me those titles.

I can't tell you how many times I've been there, totally exhausted, with my motorcycle upside down in a creek. And I still have to get up this rock face and you're going straight up and there's another rock and you're looking up at it and you're exhausted. I have to remember other people have done it, so it can be done. It's a matter of deciding you can do it and then doing it.

One of the things that taught me best was a motorcycle crash. I had a very generous sponsor who had never seen me race, so he came out to watch me. This race started on a motocross track, which I'm not good at. And there were some fast women there. I got the hole shot and was doing really well for the first two laps, but he wasn't there yet. The next time, he was there, cheering me on. I came to my first corner and I just didn't take it with great style and there was this big straightaway, so I really got on the gas. In his entire time of sponsoring me he got to watch me ride for about a minute, because I went flying off the bike, skidding on the ground, and broke my shoulder.

The next two months, when I couldn't move the arm, were a really black time for me. I was really struggling with my emotions, because it was the first thing that ever went that wrong for me in my entire life. I've been blessed. Physical stuff is really important in my life. I just love to move. You can't stop me. But I went through that fear and hopelessness, and came out of it. I was a lot better equipped when the cancer diagnosis came. I had learned a lot about dealing with fear.

In September of 2003, we rode down to Central America and we came back in time for my hysterectomy, which led to the cancer diagnosis. Those bikes just sat there for a while because everything got topsy-turvy. I've chosen an alternative therapy for my cancer treatment and my medications are complicated.

A couple of days before the diagnosis, I'd bought a new street bike I named Bella. During that awful time, vacillating between hope and despair, riding through the countryside with Bella would consistently bring me peace, joy and hope and show me the present moment was the most precious. I rode quickly, picturing myself outracing the cancer cells.

Seven weeks after my surgery and three weeks after my diagnosis, my partner wanted to go down to an enduro in the States. I was feeling good enough to ride, so we went with a friend and her boyfriend, both superb riders. The enduro route was terrible, all muddy and rooty and my bike wasn't running well. I would get stuck and the bike would die and she and I would kick it and we'd get going again and then I would get stuck again. I think we had houred out of this race before even an hour had passed. At some point, she suggested we try to find a nice way back, because we'd already been riding a couple of hours and were all covered in mud and exhausted. When I got back, I realized I hadn't thought about cancer for about four hours. It was like — "I can do this!" When I ride, everything is good. Even if it's bad, even if you're stuck in mud up to your seat, it is still good.

My oncologist wanted me to do whole-pelvis radiation. Radiation has to be done within a certain time frame if it's going to help at all. I am an epidemiologist but I've taught graduate courses in medical-decision making, so I'm not an easy patient to have. It was a rare cancer and I think I knew more about it in a week than my oncologist did. From everything I read, I didn't really feel the radiation was going to help more than it was going to harm, but I was having trouble deciding because he was really pushing it.

A really good friend of mine said, "Let's just go canoeing for a few days. You really need to get away from this. When you come back, you give him your answer." So three other women and I went on this canoe trip at a remote island. Every day I would walk up to a small lake and I would meditate and try and let the answer come to me. It was down to the last day and I still hadn't decided. So I went up by the lake and spent a few hours there. When I came back, it was almost dark and they'd already made the campfire. They were all looking at me. "So did you come to a decision?" "Yup. I'm going to win the enduro championship this year. That's what I want to do." Which meant, of course, I couldn't do the radiation, because the championship would be in the same time period. That was a tough one to win.

In 2008 we finally decided we would go on a proper trip with the bikes and then sell them. (They are both still riding.) Bicyclists have put together an off-pavement route from Banff to Mexico. It crosses the Continental Divide about twenty-six or twenty-seven times. We started in the snow in late September and it was just so stunningly beautiful. You think, it can't get better than this, and then you crest the next ridge and have this completely different panorama. It's rife with wildlife — the bears, big-horn sheep and antelope. We even had good coffee and food most of the time.

At times, I was completely terrified. During a pretty treacherous downhill, I lost my nerve and sat down. My front wheel was on this big rock, but now I was stopped and I had no momentum to get over it. I had made the situation a lot harder than it needed to be. So, a few days later, we were on a six kilometer stretch with a really steep downhill angle, all loose boulders and a cliff off to the side. My partner was up ahead and I thought, "I know he's not terrified but I am." I knew I couldn't succumb to it, because once you do sit down, you're lost.

Some things are certainly beyond my skill level, but more often it's something just at the very outer limit of my skill level, so I can get through it, although I can't get through it if I'm afraid or I talk myself out of it. I've learned to take a deep breath and remember that, if the fear takes over, you actually can't get through. But if you learn to compartmentalize fear or anger, you recognize you're afraid, but you can put it over in some other section of your being and keep moving ahead.

Meg's Ride is an annual trail ride for women started by fellow riders to raise funds for local cancer facilities. A lot of women don't ride a lot and this is a big day for them.

A couple of years ago, the weather is miserable — sleet and snow. Another woman and I get to the lunch stop first, and you see these women coming in who don't ride that often, and they are all happy. This is something they couldn't have imagined doing before and they are doing it and they're doing it together. It's so beautiful to see. It is the sense of empowerment that makes it for them. I'm not really a good example of somebody who was empowered by the motorcycle, but I think I already was empowered and then I embraced it through motorcycling.

One thing I got from my father is that you have to be aware of the gifts you didn't have to work for, and try to maintain some humility about that. I was raised in an environment where I was encouraged to take risks and given the opportunity to do so. I happen genetically to be very blessed physically. I just started racing duathalons this summer and I won most of them at age fifty-four. So, if I can inspire someone, I mean, if that's a gift I can give to them, then great, I've given back a little bit.

When my cancer came back for the third time, I was told, "You're out of here." You really start looking for the miracles, just to know they exist. Now I spend an inordinate amount of time trying to help people find a path. I met a friend at a ride this fall who had lost his daughter to cancer the year before and I had spent some time counseling them through it. He asked me how I was doing. "Things are great. I started racing duathalons this summer and to my amazement I won several of them, so I'm totally into it." "Really? You're feeling one-hundred percent again?" "Yes." Then he reminded me that, only a year ago, I had said I had to accept that I would never come back one hundred percent physically. At some point in the winter, I had forgotten about that. So, now I had something else to celebrate again.

Kelly Patterson McGrath

Occupation: entrepreneur, researcher and follower of her heart
Location: Barrie, Ontario
Age: 47
Riding Discipline: street
Began Riding: 2001
Website: leadforwomen.com

Kelly is a gifted trainer, facilitator and speaker. She has a natural ease and calm demeanor that creates an open, comfortable atmosphere as soon as you meet her. I was compelled to meet her after I discovered her line of stylish T-shirts, note cards and journals for women riders.

Professionally, she has launched a series of workshops to inspire, empower and motivate women. She is the author of a Leadership for Women research project and focuses on initiatives to enable women to become better leaders. Recently she decided to share the mind and body changing world of Pilates and fitness with others.

My husband always wanted a motorcycle and finally got his license eighteen years ago. We'd just been married and had four small children, two of his and two of mine. Fifteen years later, he still didn't own a motorcycle and his practice of dragging me to see motorcycles was starting to drive me nuts. Every weekend he wanted to go to the dealer, just to sit on them, walk around, touch them. I traveled a lot for business at the time and one day when I was in Atlanta, I received a call saying, "Honey, I am sitting on a lovely green-eyed lady." He bought a motorcycle that was an incredible green and very beautiful. He was very excited and I was very excited for him.

We started going for rides and eventually wanted to ride it out to the country to visit my folks and show my dad. Here we were, an inexperienced rider, me hanging on for dear life, high winds, gravel road and a bike that was beautiful but top heavy and not the easiest to handle. My dad didn't say much other than, "My dad never let me have a motorcycle. That's really nice."

Leaving was more of an adventure. As my husband took off, the rear tire slid sideways, the bike fell over and I sailed into the ditch. The first thing he said to me was, "Get up! Get up! Hurry up and help me get this bike up." He didn't ask me how I was or whether I was OK. "Your dad might be watching at the window. Hurry up." Thank God they weren't looking out the window because they would have had a fit.

That was a turning point for me. I needed to be in control and in charge of my own motorcycle. I signed up for the course the next week and I never got on the back of his bike again. I had to have the power. I have to be in charge of my life. I have to be in charge of where I'm going on the road and if I fall, then it's my fault and nobody else's.

I loved the actual physical power of the bike. I'm just finding out in my later life that I'm a massive science brain. I love the way engines work and I love the whole science of it, so the power of it for me was the actual physical power of the bike and how it can take me forward, and that was really what was driving me. I wanted to have one of those between my legs and be in control.

When I go on my bike, it's about connection with nature and how I connect with the world around me. The sounds, the smells — and that's a seasonal thing, so we're very lucky to have seasons here in Canada — particularly the smells are so intense. The farmers are plowing the fields for seeding, for instance, and you get the smell of that earth, that air, or the manure or the fresh-cut hay. For me, it's a connection to nature, to the earth, and it's a very emotional experience.

One of the lessons I've learned is it's okay for me to be in control and not feel that I'm bossy, pushy, a bitch or any of those things. It's okay for me to feel comfortable in my own power. Having conquered riding a motorcycle and having that power beneath me has enhanced it even further.

When I see another woman rider, I'm very connected with that energy. Looking at her or talking to her in her state of confidence, I can see how much it's risen. On the other side, I have seen women who have been forced to ride a motorcycle by their partners. They're not comfortable and they're not happy. The whole point is not whether you do or don't ride. It's that you need to make that decision, not anybody else. That's part of the confidence and that's part of the power.

When I do workshops and training with women, it's about letting them decide where they need to go and what they need to do. Not because society or their partners dictate it or they think they have to, but because they've chosen to. That's very different from doing something you think you can do to stretch. We all need to stretch in order to build our character, in order to cross that bridge to see where it will take us. But there's that fine line between getting on a motorcycle because you really want to conquer your fear and *you* really want to get that power, versus doing it because somebody's telling you to.

I want women to feel they can step out, step forward, be confident, stop questioning what they're doing and do it. Too often we seek approval to do what we need to do. Too often we take things personally. In the leadership research I'm doing, one of the things that comes up more often than not with these women in power, women in leadership positions — they take things too personally. That's why they can't move forward. It's not about you, so put it aside, let it slide off.

Women are great multi-taskers and motorcycling requires multi-tasking to the limit. We're looking at the ground for holes, we've got to look ahead, we've got to look sideways, we've got to make sure we're changing gears. It's a multi-sensory experience and it's hard. It's stressful. When you get back from a ride you're tired, because you spent so much time and energy with your brain as well as your body.

I think everybody should try riding a motorcycle. It's an incredible source of power and energy. But if it's not for you, that's all right, too. The whole point is you need to do what you need to do. You know, we can do anything we choose to.

Ila Sissons

Occupation: healing arts — spiritual and emotional counseling, Bowen physical therapy, author
Location: Orangeville, Ontario
Age: 59
Riding Discipline: street
Began Riding: 1998
Website: circleofchange.ca

As soon as I saw Ila, I gravitated toward her. When I heard her speak, she had the voice of an angel. Ila is a healer and after she touched me, I was convinced she was an angel.

A local whole-foods store was celebrating its thirtieth anniversary by hosting a number of alternative-therapy practitioners in a tent set up in the parking lot. I was making the rounds, looking for anyone who could help me get my shoulder back into shape.

I followed up with a visit to her office, where she shared facilities with her husband, a family practitioner. I was intrigued to discover that, like me, they were both interested in the work of Carolyn Myss and had attended her workshops. And they both rode motorcycles!

When my husband got a bike almost eleven years ago, I was on the back of it. One ride and I said, that's it, I'm getting my own bike. I'm sorry I waited so long to find all those wonderful feelings I could have had for another twenty or thirty years of my life.

When I was still a brand new rider, we set off on a ten thousand kilometer cross-country trip. We had hail, thunderstorms, lightning — like a right-in-your-face storm on a flat road where there was nothing and no place to hide away. We had every type of road condition. In Minnesota, we had a thirty-five mile detour, all on gravel. In Yellowstone National Park, we had mud — slick, greasy mud — and I had never experienced that before.

I knew the power to deal with these situations was in me, but it doesn't always come out. Until we're tested, we're not always sure of what's there. I did assume right from the beginning I'd get home safely.

We headed through Minnesota, South Dakota and Wyoming on our way to the mountains and the Great Divide. I love nature and when I ride, it's like I'm being kissed by it and I love that.

But we had come all this time, heading for the Great Divide, heading for the mountains, and I was carrying a lot of fear. I had never ridden in big mountains and all I could think of was these big drop-offs.

Finally, though, the moment arrived when I took a big, deep breath and I could feel myself relax and look up. I came to the knowing that there wasn't room for me and fear on the bike. One of us had to get off. I saw that majestic view of the mountains with snow on them, and from then on everything was so beautiful. We were really high up and it was still like spring up there. We passed a waterfall and I could feel the mist on my face. Everything was so alive.

The day I realized that, it was as though nothing, nothing, can transplant fear into me. Fear helps me pay attention, but then it's gone. Physical things can happen to me, and that's where the fear runs when I'm on my motorcycle. If it wants to get me, it will get me on what could happen to my physical body. But when I transfer it, it's not just my physical world where I perceive fear. It can be emotional. It can be even spiritual. Fear is fear. So I've come to perceive it much more quickly and I know whatever aspect of my being it's knocking on my door to get into, it's the same thing. I've learned so much from my bike, and the realization of being in fear and dealing with it is certainly one of them. When I came back from that trip, I stood so tall.

I often say to people, if you want to know how to do something effectively, you have to practice. Now, when it's a new situation I'm going into on my motorcycle, and I recognize that feeling of fear, I just simply say, you know, one of us has to get off.

One time, the road unexpectedly changed to gravel, and there it was in front of me. All I could hear was, "Don't brake. Don't brake. Just ride through it." So I stepped on the gas and just rooooooooodddddddde through it and got through to the other end. And then I thought, my God, isn't this just like life? When something awful happens, you want to put on the brakes and you want to stop it, but you learn to mooove on through.

I got those lessons so often when I was first learning to ride. It was a marvel for me, how I would learn about me and I would reinforce life lessons through the physical or the emotional lessons from my motorcycle. Now, that's a little different. When I get on my bike, it's mostly a joy, and I want all the opportunities I can get to be on it. But there are still lessons. They still come.

The real test of how good a rider you are is not how fast you can go, but how fast you can stop. I like to ride with that always in the front of my mind. The power of the bike is very humbling. With all that power, with the balance of the bike, I keep it on the road, I keep it upright. But I'm very respectful of what it takes to stop a bike, especially in bad conditions. The wisdom comes from knowing how to stop it when it's full force, when I've got a situation to deal with.

I have a whole thing I do when I get out on my bike to ride. I call on the Diva of motorcycle riding, because I want everything to be protected. I understand the energy of my motorcycle as though it's made of the elements of heaven and earth, and everything has energy, so I know the energy of my motorcycle and I know my motorcycle as a being.

There's an amazing feeling of being one. I never feel this in my car. I never feel I have this creation of metal and I'm propelled by gasoline. I don't have an experience with another machine ever that I have with my motorcycle. And it's quite amazing to feel at one with a machine. But that's part of what I love about riding, to feel myself melded into this metal being. When you're learning, you don't have that experience because you're still learning the skills. Once you've mastered those and learned not to take fear as a passenger, you can move to that place.

We can call things that we know inside us, and they speak to us. But when you get a chance to speak it to someone else, to hear yourself and to be heard, it's a whole other level of knowing. It's beautiful to journey back into my years of riding. I don't have those stories from my car. They have not imprinted in the same way as they have from my motorcycle.

The difference between walking or a bicycle and a motorcycle is very much about speed and how you feel the elements. There's a rushing when I feel the wind on my body. I didn't know I loved speed until I got my motorcycle. I know that's a part of it for me. Even in a convertible, it's not the same. On a motorcycle, your whole body, except for what you sit on, is in some way exposed to the wind and to the elements. It's an absolutely clear connection.

CHAPTER 7

Discovering and Using Your Power

"Once you know facing your fear is going to bring so many rewards, you just keep facing your fear."

—Writer Carla King

EVERY MOTORCYCLE HAS POWER BANDS, the operating-speed range where the engine is running most efficiently to produce the power needed for the situation. The rider needs to use the power in one band before shifting gears or the motorcycle will get bogged down and lose momentum. Applying this notion to other life situations requires practice and discipline. We need to understand how much personal power we have and use it wisely. Giving power away to fear and negative emotions means it won't be there when we need it.

If we use our control inappropriately, we can run into trouble — with or without the bike. Failing to understand where our power band is, letting go of the clutch too soon and applying the brakes incorrectly are all actions that can cause us to lose control. To think about it simplistically, the power from the engine is transferred to the rear wheel, which then moves us forward. If we think about the front wheel in terms of our fears, we can recognize giving the rear wheel more power will continue to move us forward and push us through our fears. There's lots of power there. We just have to use it.

The years 2006 and 2007 were an expansionary period for me. My touring business was beginning to take hold. I had new friends and a network of new business associates. I began to get involved with women's programs from several large motorcycle manufacturers. I was serving with a national advocacy organization. And I was having a lot of fun.

Still, I struggled with self-confidence and wondered whether I was doing the right thing. Why wasn't my business taking off more? Why didn't I have the relationship I wanted? Things weren't happening fast enough for me.

New doors were opening, though. Ontario Tourism was beginning to actively market motorcycle tourism. I had enlisted several friends to go on a scouting trip to northern Ontario, looking for routes and tour ideas. It so happened that along the way we were invited to participate in a photo shoot Ontario Tourism was conducting. That was the beginning of a mutually beneficial relationship that continues to grow.

My goal with Trillium was to deliver an experience, not merely lead people around, so I began to offer Do-It-Yourself motorcycle maintenance workshops. It's amazing to see how quickly people become engaged. Invariably, at least one motorcycle arrives in an unsafe condition, its rider completely oblivious to worn-out tires, incorrect chain tension, loose parts, frayed cables or low air pressure in the tires.

Initially, I taught women only, but calls started coming in from men. Now the ratio is almost fifty-fifty. That's an indication of how far women have come in motorcycling, but also of how men have evolved. When Trillium started, an acquaintance said, "You'll never get men to follow you around." Not only do they follow me around, they pay to do it. And now, they come to my maintenance workshops. A great sign of the times.

That same year, with the full support of the MCC board of directors, the Women Riders Council was formed. I was thrilled to be a part of this because it so perfectly aligned with my vision.

My interest in writing a book kept percolating to the surface. I attended a week-long creative writing course before I even understood what creative writing was. The Arts School was in the heart of some of the best riding in Ontario, so when school was out for the day, I was able to enjoy some spectacular scenery. That was the perfect complement to the lessons and a certain creative synergy blossomed that couldn't have grown so effectively any other way.

One day, I headed down "Airport Road" to the end of the pavement and a grass strip with a couple of small planes sitting on it, evidently the airport. The road continued as packed gravel, which wouldn't be suitable for my tours, but it intrigued me, so I continued.

The road soon degraded into potholes, erosion ruts and gravel the texture of marbles. The low hardwood-tree canopy created a verdant tunnel of green. It was beautiful, but my bike wasn't designed for this kind of riding. I was past the point of no return, though. Aside from the personal risk, I had my laptop on board, and rightly or not, I considered it more fragile than I was, and I sure didn't want to crash and lose everything on it. A rutted side road appeared through the trees and I had no choice but to take it. The continuation of the road I was on was washed out and impassable. No one, including me, knew where I was. I had no cell phone reception, I was navigating treacherous conditions and I kept thinking about the bears that inhabited these woods, probably watching me.

I did the only thing I knew to do: calmed my mind, stood on the footpegs, kept my eyes focused on where I wanted to go and kept my speed up. After a few more blind corners, the road opened up and rough pavement appeared, now hugging the shoreline of a beautiful northern lake. The sense of accomplishment and peace I felt as I enjoyed the serenity and beauty was magnified by the relief of making it through thirty kilometers of bush. It made excellent fodder for my writing the next day.

My personal road was subtly and naturally changing direction and opening up exponentially as I followed my inner guidance system, buoyed by a sense of harmony. My life was rich, vibrant, full of momentum and energy. I was enjoying the flow, even if the loose-gravel shoulders seemed a little frightening. If I stayed on course, I would stay off those shoulders.

I decided it was time to leave my haven of the past four years, and I found another country home where I would live in a loft over a garage. It seemed symbolic that I'd stepped out, come out from underground.

I made a conscious decision to spend more time on my own. I needed to recharge my batteries but I also realized I needed to come to terms with understanding and loving who I was more if I was to be of any use to anyone else. I discovered how nurturing time alone can be and came to enjoy my own company. I learned there was no point in going out merely to avoid being "alone." That's when I get into trouble and surround myself with the wrong people, who are also trying to avoid being alone.

The women whose stories are included in this chapter found the power to conquer fear and are living proof the rewards are far greater than the fear itself. Those rewards often appear in unusual and unexpected ways, but we have to be out there, challenging ourselves, for the rewards to come to us. They're not going to appear while we're at home in front of the television.

Carla King

Occupation: writer, adventurer, world traveler
Location: San Francisco, California
Age: 50
Riding Discipline: Adventure
Began: 1972
Website: CarlaKing.com

Carla says that facing your fear brings so many rewards you'll just keep facing your fear. She learned that by doing it.

Carla lives a life most of us only dream of. Dealing with a troublesome situation in her early twenties shaped the rest of her life. Her then-husband failed to join her on a much anticipated trip through Europe and she found herself alone in Italy with a motorcycle. Give up, or go on? It turned out to be the first of many solo travels all over the world, on often unreliable indigenous motorcycles, among them Urals, Moto Guzzis, Chang Jiangs and Enfields. She recently rode from the Austrian Alps to the Sahara Desert in Morocco.

Already a writer, Carla began to specialize in motorcycle adventure travel, authoring the Motorcycle Misadventures series of travelogues of real-time journals from the road, articles and books. Her writing has been published in motorcycle magazines and travel anthologies including Wild Writing Women: Stories of World Travel, *many editions of* Travelers' Tales *anthologies, and* In Search of Adventure. *Her book,* American Borders: Breakdowns in Small Towns All Around the USA, *chronicles her journey test riding a Ural sidecar rig for the American market. A story from her upcoming book* The China Road Motorcycle Diaries *is included in* Travelers' Tales Best Travel Writing 2011: True Stories from Around the World. *She and I are the only two people I know who don't watch television.*

I grew up in North Carolina farm country. As a restless fourteen year old, I suddenly saw the rusty old motorcycle in our garage as a getaway vehicle. My dad and I fixed it together, and suddenly I was free. I'd ride out past the fence, through the orchard and past the pond, down trails next to tobacco fields and into the woods.

Because I was raised in the country, vehicles have always been a part of my life, so they've never been threatening to me. I realize now that my early training as a farm girl was a valuable, rare gift most women don't get. It released a lot of fears and created a self-sufficiency I think of as a building block.

I was twenty-four when I married a man who seemed to share my desire to travel, but four long years passed before we made real plans to go. Once the date was set, the arrangements were left to me, as my husband was busy with a big project at work. I rented two Honda 750's to be picked up in Milan, made lists of gear and bought guidebooks, phrasebooks and detailed maps to plan our route. But when it came time to book the trip, he backed out.

I was angry and disappointed because we hadn't taken a real vacation in four years — since our honeymoon. Also, because we had been dreaming of this trip since we had been dating, and it had been delayed too many times.

Of all my emotions, anger won out. I booked my own airline ticket, then presented him with the itinerary and motorcycle rental agency information so he could make his own arrangements. He conceded that he might join me for the last two weeks of the trip, if the project was completed. He didn't try to talk me out of going, or suggest a new date that would be more convenient for him.

I thought he would relent, but when the day came, he drove me to the airport and I boarded the plane alone. Several hours into my flight, panic set in. Until then, anger and disappointment had obscured all other emotions, most notably, fear: fear about the future of my marriage, and fear about traveling alone.

I got off in Milan, not understanding the language, on my first motorcycle trip and alone. I could have stayed in B&Bs here and there and not done much and cried. I did that anyway. But anger and stubbornness can be a gift. After a couple of weeks I realized, "Hey, this isn't so bad after all."

Today, I thank my ex-husband for accidentally allowing me to discover my love for solo travel. It would have never occurred to me to plan a trip alone. When we're young, society imposes some pretty tight little rules about what we can and can't do. Even though it remained unsaid, it wasn't acceptable for a woman to just go off motorcycling across Europe by herself.

People sometimes say, "I could never spend that much time alone. I would just go crazy. I need to talk to somebody!" It's difficult to understand how nurturing being alone can be. How so many obstacles are removed when you rely upon your own senses. Today I find it so much easier to open up to others and the gifts that they bring because my instincts have been honed, and I trust them. Once you've experienced the rewards that come because you've faced that initial fear of diving off into the unknown, you just keep going.

Some people say, "I'm just happier when I feel safe," and I think, "Are you really happy inside that little bubble?" Sure, safety is important, but what are you missing? Are you living up to your potential? When you're traveling solo a sixth sense kicks in, maybe even a seventh. I know that we definitely have instincts, but we've suppressed them, and even premonition, and other mysterious forces without names. Recognizing these powers for the first time is a real breakthrough.

Imagine this. You ride up and take off your helmet. People see that you're a woman and they're so floored that they smile and laugh and invite you to their house. Your instincts say, yes, go. And you do, and stay, and you've gotten the huge gift of being included in a new culture, a family, of discovery. Of learning little bits of a new language. But you also realize that you are a gift. You're the circus come to town, the extended family member, the wondrous messenger from afar. That doesn't happen so much in America or Europe, but in Africa, India and Asia, it's so much fun.

All of my best experiences have happened when I'm completely broken down and helpless and somebody comes to the rescue. Then I get to stay in somebody's home in China or India or Canada, seeing what people really do all day, what they really eat, go shopping with them, take care of the baby, and participate in their life. It's why I love riding around the world on rickety motorcycles that are quite sure to break down. It creates the opportunity to contribute to the world, to let people know that somewhere, far, far away, there are other people like me, open and friendly, with families and friends and lives that are so much like theirs.

I also love travel for its opportunity to become completely immersed, to get away from the petty distractions and worries that come with living in a routine. When traveling, you're pretty much occupied with the basics of food, clothing and shelter. Fuel for the motorcycle. Staying warm or cool. Those delicate tendrils of instinct and premonition are fully activated and you're living in the moment, trusting them, and letting them guide you.

I love camping out but the biggest reason I take camping gear on my trips is that I hate to be locked into an itinerary. If I've planned my trip so thoroughly that I know every road, every sightseeing detour, every hotel, there's no opportunity for serendipity, to take that intriguing road off in the other direction, or to say "yes" to an invitation.

I'm convinced that, in this era of self-sufficiency and isolation, something in our DNA is not being satisfied and we unconsciously crave to help others. We can be interdependent in this kind of world. In this era, where community has been downgraded, where so many of us live isolated and self-sufficient lives in our suburban homes, we've lost something. We've lost the town square and the barn raisings and harvesting. That basic need to gather, to help one another, is not being fulfilled.

Motorcycling has allowed me to take a lot more risks in other areas of my life, too. As a freelance writer my employment is not guaranteed. I write articles and books, and contract with small and large companies to do publishing and technology projects. I've been thrilled to experience moments in history like the crazy days of multimedia and the 90's era rave scene and the early days of Burning Man and San Francisco literary life and other "edgy" social circles and friends. Breaking out of stereotypes has helped me not to put people in categories, to stereotype them, maybe because I hate being stereotyped so much.

People tell me I'm brave or courageous. But I'm not brave. I've just learned how to overcome my fear. Courage isn't about the lack of fear. It's about the willingness to overcome it. Curiosity helps, too. You know how people who are curious and following a thread are so attractive? I think it's an aura, one of those invisible powers like instinct and premonition. You become more of a person of interest, exuding the power of an independent person rather than being led about as a tourist.

I see parallels between understanding the mechanical power of a motorcycle and understanding personal power. The most obvious is that if you understand the workings of your machine and the workings of your body, and if you know how to maintain them both, you're much better off. You are attuned to how things are sounding and feeling. I know when my motorcycle is not feeling well.

When I told people I was going to ride through China with a rickety old sidecar, just two people said, "You are going to have the best time!" The rest of them said things like, "Oh, my God, aren't you scared?" "What if you get malaria and food poisoning?" "What if somebody robs you?" "What if you get in an accident?"

It's important to know that the world is a safe, wonderful place and fantastic stuff is going to happen. I prefer to listen to my own voice.

Tigra Tsujikawa

Occupation: marketing manager, American Motorcyclist
Association (AMA)
Location: southern California
Age: 45
Riding Discipline: off-road, street
Began: on-road 1985; off-road riding/desert racing 2003

Tigra is insightful, persistent and committed to her goals. Above all, she's a person of integrity, inner strength and dedication to furthering the interests of all riders.

As AMA's marketing manager, you can find her at the Vintage Motorcycle Days, International Women's Conferences, Hall of Fame events and Motorcycle Trade Shows across the United States, at AMA Headquarters in Ohio — and sometimes at her home in California.

Approaching my fortieth birthday, I began to question my ability for physical accomplishments. Granted, I was recovering from a fractured femur, but I was not prepared for that sudden erosion of confidence. I decided I was going to surf and go back to off-road riding. The insights, strength and confidence I've gained have been invaluable, in riding and other areas of my life.

I had always been intrigued by motorcycles, but I actually got into riding because I needed cheap transportation. I come from a traditional Japanese-American family, and my dad was not very happy with the choice his youngest child, a daughter, had made. It didn't help any that I had a cousin who was paralyzed from a slow-speed accident and a boyfriend Dad didn't like. But I had always broken the mold we were raised in.

Five days after my boyfriend started teaching me how to ride, we took a six-hour trip to Spokane from Seattle. I didn't have the proper experience or gear, and I didn't have a good partner. I wasn't prepared for the physical and emotional drains, so I found the ride extremely difficult. But I made it back safely with me and my bike intact, and a whole new respect for the sport.

I developed an avid interest in off-road riding in my late thirties. Short rides progressed to five-day rides with friends and Hare and Hound races[8]. Then, three years into it, I had the accident that broke my femur. I didn't really feel the pain and thought it was a charlie horse. When they wouldn't let me get up and I realized I was in the hospital and couldn't walk, I was shocked. It was the first time I ever experienced not being able to do something I put my mind to. I started to doubt myself, my skills and my ability. My self-confidence disappeared, not just for riding but in pretty much everything I was doing. But just like I learned to get up and get the right gear on the street part of riding, I learned the skills to get back on the bike off-road.

The trip I did last Christmas is evidence of how far I've come. Together with my boyfriend, I rode fourteen hundred miles off-road in Baja. It was the sum of every situation I'd been in during seven years of off-road riding: the terrain, falling down and getting up, being tired, being so excited about what I was doing and having that high level of energy.

My accomplishments on the motorcycle, whether it's street or off-road, have really given me strength. The kind of excursions I've done have not been easy. The confidence they have given me help me every day. Throw me a challenge and I know I can get through it. I can evaluate a situation, decide what needs to be done and execute. That's exactly what I've learned I can do on a motorcycle.

Riding gives me perspective. I know that when I'm really stressed out I need to get out and ride and remember what's important, what real beauty is and how concerns that seem huge when you're sitting at your desk are really quite small. It's also taught me people are generally

---

[8]   Dirt bike race consisting of two forty-mile loops over natural, rugged terrain, typically held in the desert.

very good and thoughtful. Meeting countless other motorcyclists on the road, at conventions or on the trail has changed my impression of people and restored my faith in mankind. Bikers are great people!

Women riders in particular impress me with their courage. It takes courage for men, too, but for women it takes more inner strength. In my generation, it was still perceived as odd for women to be riding motorcycles. Knowing about the others gave me extra encouragement and inspiration. As riders now, we need to encourage and inspire other women, not only in motorcycling but in all those things they may be a little apprehensive about trying. It may be motorcycling or surfing or competing in karate, like I did. Being there for each other makes us all stronger and more confident.

Kellee Irwin

Occupation: vice president, Insurance Corporation of British Columbia
Location: Vancouver, British Columbia
Age: 44
Riding Discipline: off-road, street, dual-sport
Began Riding: as a child

Kellee grew up in a motorcycling family and attributes her career success to the skills she developed through trail riding. I have been honored to know Kellee and work with her through her role with the Women Riders Council of the MCC and as President of the Canadian Motorcycle Hall of Fame and Museum Foundation.

To call her energized would be a gross understatement. She serves on the boards of the American Association of Motor Vehicle Administrators (Region IV) and the Women in Insurance Cancer Crusade (B.C.). She is a former president of the British Columbia Safety Council. You try and keep up with her!

Her success in driving significant project and/or process improvement within her organization has earned her industry respect. Last September, she was the first Canadian to win one of Insurance Networking News' four Women in Insurance Leadership Notable Achievers awards.

I grew up in a male-dominated industry without ever feeling any barriers in it because I was female. I was treated as an equal. I was twelve when I started working at Irwin's motorcycle shop, a family business that has been around since the thirties so I literally did grow up with it and always had a choice about riding. I started racing and doing trials when I was fourteen, retired when I was nineteen, and started racing again at thirty, although I don't race anymore.

One of the important things when you're developing your corporate career, and I think motorcycling gave me the confidence to
do this, is the passion for life. Riding is the one thing I do when I
don't think about work, because you can't. When you're riding, you
have to be one hundred percent focused for me.

When I went into the insurance industry twenty years ago, it was
largely male-dominated, but I felt comfortable in it. I had a business
degree and a lot of practical experience gained through ten years of
working part-time in the motorcycle business during high school and
university. It helped me develop people skills and practical business
skills, so that kind of gave me a leap start. I was very comfortable
with either clients or teams that were all male other than me. Today,
I'm the youngest member of the executive committee and younger
than the average of our extended executive.

Motorcycling throughout my corporate career has actually built a
bit of a brand for me. I'm very open about what I do, and very proud.
We put together some pictures for presentations to our key business
brokers and our distributors, and mine is me with a dirty face and
helmet head, smiling in Baja.

Riding a motorcycle taught me to manage risk. Now, I manage
risk for a living. I need to be aware of hazards and make very quick
decisions when I'm riding. How fast do you go around a corner if you
don't know what's around the corner? As another example, I have no
desire to ride my street bike in downtown Vancouver, just because
I know of statistics and intersection crashes and managing speed.

It really has taught me about teamwork. When someone is on a
trail and their bike's broken down or there's an injury or something's
happened, it's about working together to make sure the person's safe.
When you're on a trail and when you're riding in Nevada or Baja, you're
looking after each other and you know all of you have to get to the
finish line safely and in one piece. And usually you get into situations
where individually you'd have a really hard time but as a team you
can get through some really hard stuff together. Maybe that's why I

did a lot of cross-country and not a lot of out-and-out racing. People I meet on adventure rides tend to become friends for life.

You don't meet too many unhappy people on a motorcycle. They have a passion for life, to live life, to explore that sense of adventure, and I think it bonds all of us in different ways.

One of the reasons motorcycling is so empowering for women is because historically it's been a male sport. And once you get empowered, that is a positive influence in a lot of different ways. I've seen women when I was teaching with the Canada Safety Council who would be really nervous and you'd see their confidence grow throughout the course. I would just want to hug them and say I was so proud of them.

I really think my role, whether on the Women Riders Council or just as an experienced woman rider is to help people when they first come into the sport. A lot of times on trail rides, if I see a woman who's nervous or doesn't have a lot of experience, I'll make a point of going over and talking to her to help make her feel more comfortable, to make sure she's okay. I know what it takes to get there. It's easier not to do it than to do it. A lot of times, people are discouraged from riding because it's too high risk, and granted, it can be intimidating. I say, good for you. You wanted to ride and you're out doing it.

I'm forty-four years old, I'm in a VP position, I have a three-digit staff managing a ten-digit portfolio. I don't think I would be as successful as I am today had I not been a rider. Riding a motorcycle makes you unique. People remember you because you ride motorcycles.

Catherine Nadeau

Occupation: dental hygienist, racer
Location: Saint-Bernard, Quebec
Age: 31
Riding Discipline: street, road racing
Began Riding: 1998

Dental hygienist by weekday, championship motorcycle racer by weekend. You never know who's cleaning your teeth!

When I first spoke with Catherine, she and her partner were expecting their first child. She has now set aside her racing goals and accomplishments to focus on raising their son.

Catherine started riding to follow a dream, and discovered she was a racer. Her competitive spirit clearly shone through as we were talking. She rose rapidly to the top of her class, competing against women, and then moved into competitions with men. An injury sidelined her — but only for a while and it only made her a stronger competitor.

I got a fourteen-year-old motorcycle in 1998 with my first paycheck and began riding on the street. I'd always dreamed of having one and now I did. In 2000, I attended my first racing school and fell in love with the track.

In 2001 and 2002 I did a lot of track days in Saint-Eustache in Montreal and St. Croix in Quebec. When *le Trophée Feminine*, a class for women, was started in 2003, it was an opportunity to race just with females. I thought, good! It's my time to start racing. That first year, we had six races in Quebec and I won all six of them.

In 2004, I began to race with the men and finished first in Quebec in the Amateur 600. In 2005 I got a new sponsor and they lent me a bike for the first five races of Women's Cup. I won everything. After that I began to race the Nationals with the men.

I crashed at Calgary in the second Nationals and my season was done. I broke my ankle, my collarbone and my back. But I knew I had to get back on the track as soon as possible to avoid losing my skills, and confidence. I started racing again six weeks later. Every time the bike leaned a little bit, I was afraid, but I wanted to show that, yes, I crashed, but I want to race again. I was able to do that. It was another side of racing, because I finished as the last girl, behind everybody. I learned I need to be patient.

It was hard. People were wondering aloud why Catherine Nadeau wasn't winning. "She's in pain." "She's afraid of the track." It was hard to hear their comments. In my mind, it was great to be on the bike and to be around the track. I wanted to regain my confidence as soon as possible and race well in 2006.

It's a long time between seasons and I didn't want to be scared the next year, so I went to Florida and did some track days for training in March, 2006. I just needed to ride. I rode and I rode and I rode, and I don't know how, but it came back.

In 2006 I won the Women's Cup and finished tenth in the Amateur 600 Nationals. I finished fourth in the Amateur 600 at Shannonville and I broke five lap records, one for the men and four for the women. It was nothing special, but I had a good season.

In 2007 Pascal Picotte lent me a bike. I finished second at the nationals at Mont Tremblant. It was a great season beginning because it was the first time in twenty-two years a girl put a foot on the podium at the Nationals.

I *love* to race. I love to be on the track. I set goals and I have to achieve them. I have to push myself every time, every lap, and that gives me a lot of power. It's the food I need. Last summer, I didn't race because I was pregnant and it was hard to be around the track because there is so much energy there.

When I finished second at Shannonville, the stands were full of people. As I got off the track, I noticed the standing ovation and then I realized it was for me. I thought, "Wow, for me?" It was good. I did so well and I got what I wanted, to finish third in the Amateur 600. I wanted people to know the girls can do well with the men and I wanted to prove I can do it, and I did that.

My toughest time was when I crashed. It was hard just to walk. I could not go to sleep alone.

I try every time to be good just to prove that, yes, I'm a girl, and I can be good. A girl *can* ride a bike properly.

My parents instilled strength in my sister and me. They gave us a lot of responsibility and independence. I lost my mother when I was nineteen and after that I felt I had to take my life and do something with it that I could be proud of, and my mother too. I like to have challenges and push myself. I do the same thing with my work.

I don't have an exciting job. I'm a dental hygienist. I want to be good and continuously learn and improve. I work for an orthodontist and you don't learn that at school. You learn that on the job. I don't know what I'm going to do next, but now I know almost everything in this job.

It's crazy how motorcycling has changed my life. Because I won races, people's views changed. Especially with young girls and boys, I realized they looked up to me and I was a role model for them. It felt good because maybe I could make a difference to them.

It's a surprise for me, because I just wanted to race I never imagined that people could be interested in me or that I could inspire dreams or make them push themselves.

Now I'm on to my next challenge in life, raising my beautiful son. I'm so happy to have him in my life. Maybe one day he will follow in my footsteps.

Oksana Buhel

Occupation: project manager, community development
Location: Georgetown, Ontario
Age: 41
Riding Discipline: street
Began Riding: 2001

When Oksana went to Vietnam for a one-year work term, she had to learn a foreign language and culture, of course, but she also learned motorcycling is very different from motorcycling in North America. They had one thing in common: things she had considered impossible were in fact very doable.

I met Oksana when, through her role with the Canadian Off-Highway Vehicle Distributors Council (COHV), she gave a presentation to our Motorcyclists Confederation of Canada (MCC) board of directors. She was thorough and could stand up to some tough questions, responding professionally and with composure, and not backing down. I was just starting to write and knew immediately she had a story to share.

There's something rebellious and nonconformist I've always liked about riding. It's an adventure, more so than with other means of transportation. I was a passenger for a while before I got my license and wasn't comfortable there, even though my husband was a good rider. I don't like someone else in control of my destiny. Plus, the view sucked. All I saw was his big head. I kept saying I'm going to and going to, I'm going to, and I never did. Then one day, on the way home from work, I stopped and bought a motorcycle.

One day, as I was enjoying my rural commute home from university, my clutch cable snapped. I knew I'd be okay as long as I didn't have to stop or switch gears. I would have to hit it right and coast through the many intersections between me and home. I was fine until I got to one where a car was approaching and I had to stop.

A bicyclist with a cell phone came by and I called for a tow. I knew it would be a while, so rather than wait for something to happen, I decided to make it happen. I started pushing the bike and came to a house with an adjacent workshop. The man who lived there turned out to be very resourceful and spent almost two hours fixing my bike. He wasn't a biker but he knew how to assess, diagnose and come up with a solution. I cancelled the tow truck while he soldered some sort of bearings onto the cable, re-routed it somehow and then used a door jamb on the outside of the clutch case to hold everything in place and make it operational. I probably had that doorjamb on there for a couple of weeks, because I thought it was kind of cool and symbolic, the way it had been cobbled together. After that, I would wave every time I passed by. I seem to meet a disproportionate number of fabulous people.

Motorcycling has influenced every area of my life. How I am underscores how I ride and how I ride underscores who I am. They all fit together. If you're resourceful on the bike, you're resourceful with your life. It has always been there for me. It just comes up with the riding. It has also taught me how little I really need to get by. You can be much more minimalist when you're riding, particularly when you're going on a trip. It's figuring out what's important and what's optional and leaving the optional behind.

In 2003 to 2004, I spent a year in rural Vietnam working with agriculture co-ops, immersed in marketing plans and a variety of activities, such as getting people organized for general assemblies, advising how the democratic process should work and learning what to consider if you're having elections. A car was available for us, but riding was the preferred method of transportation, not just because the scenery was fantastic, but also because it was often the only way to traverse the countryside.

I rode everywhere on a Minsk, a Russian motorcycle that is a mix between a trail and dual-sports bike. I'm certain it could withstand a meteor impact. They take some getting used to, but if they fall over, there's rarely any damage, and you just pick them up and get going again. Rush hour was when all the water buffalo would come in from the fields and the chickens and dogs would cover the road and you had to be so nimble.

Shortly after I arrived, our project team was invited to a commune for their general elections. Innocently, I chose to ride. What could be so different about riding here? A parade of people heading to the communes lined the way. We were riding along the river and it was sand and I fell. We went over the bridge and I fell. Next came the muddy rice fields, and I fell, this time in mud that came to mid-thigh. The locals were arriving in dress shoes and slacks, and I looked like I'd been traipsing through the jungle. They watched me fall each time, and figured by the third time I would give up. They admired my persistence, which in turn earned their respect.

Another time, I was riding to a project in another province and encountered a construction zone. It's not like construction you see here. You see piles of river rock and people beating them and lots of strenuous manual labor. The only way to get by was by leaving the road, going down a steep incline with big rocks sticking out all over the place. I remember having that feeling in my stomach and being so scared I thought I was going to cry. I could go back, but that wouldn't get me to the project, and besides, I had to overcome this challenge.

I was smoking at the time, so I got off, lit up and said to myself, okay, let's just sit here and wait and see what happens. My motto has been, when you don't know what's going on, just stop and look. No decisions, just stop and look. I watched the first person go through and they went through really easily. Then I watched as two or three more people went through. They were going right over the rocks, whereas I would have thought to stay away from the rocks and go through the mud. After three people, I said okay, if they can do it, I can do it. Let's go.

I had to forcefully relax myself, so I did that, and rode through just as I had watched them do. When I got down, I didn't care who was looking. I got off that bike, jumped around and cheered myself for making it.

Riding is still pretty much a stereotypically male-dominated hobby. It impresses me to see a woman going against the grain. One time I was taking the streetcar to work and I looked over and I saw a woman driving a fire truck and I couldn't stop myself from staring at her. She had a little smile and I could just see the pride on her face and I thought, "Right on!" If I see another woman rider, I think that woman's pretty much saying, "I tell me what to do." This is a woman who doesn't get stopped by anything she doesn't choose to get stopped by.

Personal power is really controlling your thoughts, because when you control your thoughts, then you are open to new possibilities. Your perception of any environment changes, whether it's your workplace or your home or personal, and I've really tried to do that. Everyone's got at least one thing that is their albatross. If you learn how to deal with it, then you are way better off. Some people or situations drive me bananas, but I'm not giving anyone else the power to make me happy or unhappy. That's mine.

Jennifer Robertson

Occupation: finance associate for a non-profit organization
Location: Newmarket, Ontario
Age: 51
Riding Discipline: street
Began Riding: 2002

When you see someone riding a motorcycle, the fact that she's a grand-mother hooked up to an intravenous pump isn't exactly what you expect. Jennifer, though, wasn't going to let a little challenge stop her from riding, even if she did have to plan her stops around tubing changes.

She started riding because she thought it was something she and her husband could do together. Once she got past most of the tough stuff of learning to ride, and past the difficulties of divorce, she was unstoppable on her Harley. She still has some challenges, but she knows that one day they, too, will be history.

Initially I had a sister who was riding a sport bike and another sister who was talking about it. I'm a bookkeeper and was also helping out with the HOG (Harley Owners Group) chapter. I started reading the newsletters, about the trips they did, the things they did together, and it sounded like a fun group.

I was also looking for something my husband and I could do together. I was devastated when my sister, her friend and my husband all passed the course, and I didn't. I had a brand new motorcycle sitting at home waiting for me. I made myself get on it every day and ride it to work and ride it around in the parking lot. When I went back for the retest, I passed, no problem. I had been too nervous the first time, and on the retest I just put that out of my mind and focused on how much I wanted to do it.

I was extremely nervous when I started riding. I had a brand new 750 Shadow, and every time I went to get on it, I'd be sick to my stomach. I dropped it a few times. I remember one autumn evening, though, I was riding in the country, and a flock of geese flew over. I could hear them, and at that moment, I connected with my bike, finally. I was so calm. From then on, I couldn't wait to get on it.

The next year, my husband, sister and I, on my brand new Harley Road King, took a two-week trip to Prince Edward Island. It was my most memorable trip to date. I was on dirt roads, I was in the rain and I was on twisties.

I had never traveled much and with a motorcycle I was traveling and seeing things I never experienced before. It was amazing. I had never been any farther for a holiday than North Bay to visit family.

Riding opened up a whole new life for me. It probably expedited the demise of my marriage. Even on my own, I was getting out into group rides, going on trips and seeing things I would never have seen. The first time I went up to North Bay all by myself, it was awesome. I can do this by myself! It was the first time in my life I'd ever lived alone and I knew I could do it. Riding gave me that insight. I can do things on my own and be happy. I don't have to have someone there all the time. It's nice if someone is there but it's really nice to ride alone, too.

I grew up with twelve siblings and we never went to the doctor unless something very serious happened. Last year, I stepped on a nail. It went in the bottom and out the top of my foot. I pulled the nail out, made sure my foot bled, put some peroxide and a Band-Aid on it and continued on my way. Six weeks later, I had a problem.

They put a PICC line in my arm that went under the skin into the top artery of my chest. They give me a portable pump with the antibiotics in it, computerized to deliver the correct dosage, and hooked it up around my waist.

I started feeling better, but I might be hooked up for months. I thought, "This shouldn't stop me from riding. It doesn't interfere with clutching or braking." The big concern from the doctor was what would happen if I fell off the bike. I said, "If I fall off the bike, that'll be the least of my worries, so it's not a concern." I had a good summer in the end, although I had my moments.

I did get tired of hearing them say, "We're going to take it off," and then hearing I'd have to keep it on longer. I got a little down, but I thought, I can still ride. Maybe people look at me a little weird but I can still ride. So I did.

I rode all the way to Quebec City hooked up to that portable intravenous. Every four hours, I had to change the medication bag, so I did have to ask for a couple of extra stops along the way. Still, it gave me a real sense of freedom, even though I could only be away three days because the tubing would have to be changed. But I was free. I could still get on my bike and go. It was therapeutic to get out, forget about it and ride.

It was kind of funny, too. We'd stop somewhere and people would almost cross to the other side of the street because they thought I might be contagious or something. I'm sure it helped my recovery that I didn't sit around and mope about my problems. With the bike I had something I could do.

With riding, I have to clear my mind and focus on what I'm doing. I forget about problems at work, problems with the kids or an IV, and just enjoy the ride. It's made me a stronger person in general. It's not a common female activity, although it's getting more so now. It gives me a feeling of empowerment, that I'm actually equal. I can do the same things a man can do and I can get the same enjoyment, or maybe more. I can do things on my own and I can do them well.

I have seven grandkids now and I work full time, plus I have a part-time job, which enables me to ride my motorcycle, so I don't always get to ride as much as I like, but I certainly try to.

Last summer I was on a ride in torrential downpours and the car in front of me stopped, forcing me to brake quickly. I went out of control and I'm not sure how I did it but instinctively I did everything I was supposed to do. Something takes over in those moments and it's good to know I'll do what I need to do. Now I'm really nervous about rain though and I'm having difficulty getting past it.

When I was learning to ride and getting over my initial terror, I would remind myself there's got to be something that made you think this is where you want to go, so keep going. I'll do the same now with the rain issue. It'll take time but I'll get over it. I will.

Shelly Glover

Occupation: Member of Parliament for Saint-Boniface
Location: Winnipeg, Manitoba
Age: 44
Riding Discipline: street
Began Riding: 2003
Website: shellyglover.ca

Consistent themes around Shelly and her motorcycling are courage, family and public service.

Given her daunting track record, it's interesting that her biggest fear in learning to ride was her sense of balance tied to her fear of humiliation in front of her police-officer colleagues. One would think that balancing a motorcycle was a walk in the park compared with balancing family, public service and personal time as well as she does.

Shelly was first elected to Canada's federal government in 2008, and in 2011 she became the first Conservative in history to win a second term in her Saint-Boniface riding. As well as being a Member of Parliament, she is Parliamentary Secretary to the Minister of Finance, and has previously held similar positions in the departments of Official Languages and Indian Affairs and Northern Affairs.

During the preceding nineteen years, she served with the Winnipeg Police Service in positions that included undercover work and investigations of child abuse, youth crime and gangs. She was the first female and bilingual spokesperson ever appointed by her department.

Shelly is a proud Métis[9] woman and married mother of five children.

---

[9]   A distinct aboriginal group descended from mixed First Nations and European heritage

I was afraid I wouldn't be able to maneuver a motorcycle. I thought, "My balance isn't that great. I don't know if I can do this." Nor did I want to embarrass myself in front of my male police-officer friends. I didn't want to be the girl who couldn't do it. The sense of power I felt once I realized I could actually manage the bike on my own was incredible. Conquering that fear was a proud and defining moment.

I'm equally proud of the courage other women display through riding. Over the years, through policing or volunteer work, I've seen many women who think they can't change things, they can't achieve something, they're not smart enough, they're not brave enough.

That is the same fear you have to overcome in motorcycling. I wish those women who think they aren't strong could just pick up a motorcycle, learn to ride it and be free out there on the highway. Maybe that would empower them to know that they can make other changes in their lives.

One of my most memorable rides happened the first time I rode with a group of women. As we were traveling down the highway, we were the queens of the world. All eyes were on us. It was the most incredible feeling of pride that we had these motorcycling sisters waving the flag and influencing people just by riding. There were no men. If our bikes broke down, we were in charge. It was so empowering.

That energy I get back from people is what in turn energizes me. Like victims who fall through the cracks. They're powerless, and that motivates me to say, "That's not fair!" Then I fight for their rights and to give them the power to flourish. It's a circle. What they give me, I fight for, and they get more rights. Then I hear about another person or group that has a problem and I fight for that.

My mind is working all the time, thinking about the next move or the next fight. When I ride, I can actually forget about all that. It's like taking a moment to smell the roses, to see the beauty of our country of Canada. Especially when I've a bad day. Like when the media has attributed something absolutely atrocious to me that I never said. That is when I like to say, "Okay, I need to go for a ride."

When I get off my bike, the strength I feel while riding has renewed something within me. I am rejuvenated and ready to face anything.

It's difficult to ride when I'm in Ottawa. In addition to representing my riding, I'm the Parliamentary Secretary for the Minister of Finance, so I work almost every day until 10:00 p.m. However, my friend Brian Jean (MP for Fort McMurray) has a Harley that he lets me use sometimes. Although those occasions are few and far between, they get me stoked!

When I'm in Winnipeg, I like to ride for causes, like the Ride for Dad. Many of the organizers are women I ride with or police officers, so there's a real "family" connection. We're very close. These are the same officers who helped me get started in riding and now we're doing bigger and better things with motorcycles.

Motorcycling has shown me that you can't judge a book by its cover. In my policing job, I saw many criminals who look the same as people I now ride with. Just because you wear leather, a bandanna and jeans, and maybe you have long hair or a long beard, doesn't mean you're a bad person. I have met the absolute nicest people and most diverse groups among my motorcycling friends. I so value the camaraderie and friendships I've built.

The same thing applies across the board. When you look at other people, you can't judge them by the way they look. It's destructive and an impediment to opening up what could be a very important and rewarding relationship. You've got to listen and find out about the person. The awareness I get from having all those friends, good people, judged by others who didn't know them, has been life-changing for me.

Some day, I would love to do a very long trip — two months of traveling from coast to coast, touring the country for the whole summer. I will need to wait until I'm out of Parliament. I wish everyone could experience it!

CHAPTER 8

Leading With Your Heart

*"Anything is so doable. It just takes dreaming, planning,
preparation and then going for it."*

—Legend Sue Slate

I NTUITIVELY, THROUGH THE EVENTS leading up to my impromptu
visit to the trillium patch in the spring of 2008, I knew my life
was changing. I felt even more strongly that my business needed to
change direction. What I found most rewarding was the personal
satisfaction when clients pushed their own limits and discovered a
whole new strength and enjoyment they never would have imagined.
Now it was my turn to face some major challenges.

The fork to that point had been vibrant and fulfilling — and far
from easy. When you're on a circuitous path with many uphill sections and measuring progress one step at a time, it can be difficult to
determine how far you've come. My experience in the woods initiated
a period of intense reflection on who I was and how I got to be there.

I was in denial for at least three months after I broke my shoulder.
I was told at first I had a minor break. Never mind that I could barely
move my arm. I was told and chose to believe it was minor and I'd

be back on my bike within four to six weeks. I had tours lined up and needed to lead them.

The first week post injury, I took pain pills and kept going. I would sit on my bike, my arm in a sling, look at the handlebars and will my right arm to reach out. It wouldn't budge. I couldn't even drive my own car because it had a standard transmission. My sister graciously lent me her new vehicle until I could reach across with my left hand to shift gears.

Two weeks post accident, I learned my injury was more significant. The bone in my upper arm had fragmented into five pieces. Surgery wasn't an option and I'd have to give it extra time to heal before starting physiotherapy. "When can I ride?" I asked. "You'll know when it's time," was all the doctor said.

Feeling desperately alone, broken and exhausted, I couldn't even ride to ease the pain. Hart was wonderful, but he was so far, far away and, in that pitch blackness, I pushed him away entirely. My head told me I was giving energy to a relationship that was wonderful, but wasn't right for me. If this was a time of change, and evidently it was, I might as well make it whole-scale. The ache in my heart was even greater than the pain in my shoulder.

I started to feel sorry for myself and tears came for the first time since I could remember. During the last years of my marriage, I had been too numb for tears, and since then they'd been blocked. Sometimes I would even go out for a ride and lift my visor so my eyes would water from the wind, hoping that it would prime the pump. Once it worked a little, but it was nothing to speak of.

Now the tears came, but only at night, when it was dark. I needed to grieve. I had suffered significant losses and I worried about how I was going to get through the season and whether I would ever recover.

In spite of my pitiful state, I did know in my heart I was not truly alone. I had to be patient, let my body heal and listen to and follow my inner guidance. Had I had someone close to look after and coddle me, I would not have learned lessons I needed to learn during that time.

As happens when we sit back and allow the universe to help rather than resist, support appeared in unexpected ways. Friends stepped in and led my rides while I drove the chase vehicle. You get a whole different perspective at the back of a group; you get a good take on group dynamics, skills and what actually goes on in a ride. When you are leading, you're constantly scanning your environment, knowing a group is following you and trusting your decisions. Being the sweep rider requires a whole different skill set and your view is that of one of the group. As a result, I was able to make some changes to our procedures that enhanced the riders' experiences and elevated the professionalism of our rides.

I still had lessons to learn about following intuition. One of the people who came to my aid seemed like a perfect helper. Looking for what I wanted to see rather than what was there, I ignored initial subtle warning signals. As the summer progressed, though, a pattern was growing: broken promises, excuses and empty words. More importantly, the behavior didn't fit my expectations, nor my personal and business values. My intuition had been right again.

I was angry, mostly at myself for not listening earlier and having the courage of my conviction or the confidence in myself. More importantly, it prompted me into action. Three months after my enlightening experience in the forest, it was time to get back on the bike. The doctor had been right. I knew it was time.

I gingerly maneuvered my bike out of the garage, started it up, got my gear on while the bike warmed up and took off, all by myself. I was a little apprehensive because I still hadn't recovered a lot of mobility and strength. But my bike and I had been through a lot together and it would carry me through this, too. I only went around my country block that day, but I felt liberated and whole again.

Two days later, I went on a much longer ride, and all the ideas that had been swirling around in my head came together and the concept of this book was born. It had taken a motorcycle to get me to slow down so I could hear and it took a motorcycle to get me back on track.

I was able to lead the rest of my tours of that summer and had the best season ever.

It could have been even better, in one way. I was invited to participate in organizing a motorcycle event at a prime tourist destination and offered a potentially lucrative role. Initially, it looked full of possibilities but I soon saw it didn't support my personal vision. The project wasn't about motorcycling; it was about profiting from motorcyclists. I wasn't interested.

A curious thing was happening even before I got back on my bike. I hadn't been in touch with Hart for almost three months, although I often sensed his spirit with me. I began to see his name, although it isn't a common one, in disparate places: on the chest of a mechanic's shirt at a shop in northern Ontario where we stopped to put on rain gear; as the main character in a novel I was reading — and I seldom read novels; on the back of a pick-up truck I was following; at an art show, where one of the prominent paintings was "Portrait of Hart." I took solace that he was still thinking of me and wishing me well.

My motorcycle and I were ready for a good long ride, the weather was beautiful, the leaves were changing and I wanted to see Trent and Patti. They now lived only fifteen hundred kilometers away, and their son needed to go for his first motorcycle ride. The ride through the Alleghenies was gorgeous, with the mountains resplendent in their fall wardrobe. The visit was all too short but we did manage to get rides in for both of the children.

I took a slightly different route home, through some scenic back country. I had just had a heart-warming visit with close friends and felt wonderful. When you travel alone, you meet more fascinating people than you ever would with another person, and everyone treats you so well. You never know who you're going to meet, and I expected a chance meeting on one of these kinds of days would be how I would meet the companion I knew was out there looking for me.

My route in both directions took me within two hours of Hart's place. Seeing the cutoff on the way down had been a poignant reminder of wonderful times and a very special companion. When we had parted at the end of May, we had agreed not to communicate again, both respecting that we needed to move on.

My bike thought otherwise, though. It broke down, right at the point on my path that was closest to him, just before I turned to head away. It began to bog down and lose power. It had never given me a speck of trouble in the six years and one hundred and twenty thousand kilometers we'd been together. Why now?

I got directions to the nearest Yamaha dealer and we limped there. They took a quick look, couldn't figure it out and said they could fit me into the shop, but not before the end of the week. But I had to be back in two days for a Harley-Davidson Garage Party.

I called Hart. It seemed silly not to. He would know where to find a reputable mechanic in this area. The new mechanic said the steering head bearings needed replacing. He could get the parts overnight and work on the bike the next day. Hart arrived with his trailer and insisted on transporting my bike back to the shop the next morning.

Two more mechanics looked at the bike and disagreed with the first diagnosis. They rode it around, back and forth, for a good hour, trying to figure out what was wrong. By now, I was sensing that the sputtering up and down the road was my bike laughing. It had accomplished its mission and Hart and I were together. It was Thanksgiving Day, and I couldn't have been more thankful.

The mechanics decided that, although they didn't know what was wrong, it was nothing catastrophic and my bike would get me home. It turned out to be a fouled spark plug. True, I had neglected changing the plugs according to the recommended schedule. On the other hand, they acted up just enough to detain me strategically and then see me back on my way.

In the stories that follow, you'll see what happens when we allow our hearts to guide us and surrender our fears and perception of control. Events and experiences beyond our imagination unfold and the universe supports us. We learn lessons on faith and trust and believing in ourselves.

Doris Maron

Occupation: financial planner
Location: Ponoka, Alberta
Age: 60
Riding Discipline: street
Began Riding: 1989
Website: untamedspirit.net

At fifty-two, Doris sold everything, packed up her motorcycle and took off for three years on a trip around the world. She has learned the world is out there to be explored and enjoyed, not the dangerous place we hear about on the news.

As her trip ended, she decided to write about her adventures, hoping it might inspire others to live their dreams. She urges the same thing as a speaker, and encourages others to trust the universe will provide for them, just as it has for her.

Doris has been a member of Women in the Wind and served briefly on the Women Riders Council.

Starting in elementary school, I dreamed of traveling around the world on my motorcycle. Fear kept me at home. One day, though, I woke up realizing I was already fifty-two years old and if I didn't go soon, I wouldn't be able to do it.

I grew up on a farm in Alberta, the seventh of nine children, and always wanted a motorcycle. I was probably in my teens when my oldest brother came home with one, but of course it wasn't something women did back then. When I got married, I tried to convince my husband to let me try it. I can remember in my early years of marriage almost panicking, thinking I was going to die before I had a chance to do any of the things I wanted to do. When I finally did learn to ride, I was forty-one years old and had been divorced for six years. I took the training course and loved it as much as I knew I would.

It changed my life by enabling me to feel my own sense of power, my own freedom to get out there and ride. It opened up a whole new community of people for me. I was a very quiet, shy, scared person for most of my life and motorcycling, the community of people I met and the reception I got from them opened up a whole new life for me. I'm more confident than I was way back then. We riders are a small group in relation to the population and it's almost like having a small town community, although it's not in a small town; it's worldwide. Anywhere you go, if you're with people who ride motorcycles, it's like you've known them forever.

Much of my growth in self-esteem came through the riding organizations I joined, because I was in these clubs as a single woman, not as somebody's passenger, and that was very rare. It's not something that happened immediately, but rather it grew.

Traveling the world made me realize we think we have to control everything in our lives, and we don't. We don't need to know "why" all the time. Even though I know it, I'm still learning it. I still fall back into that trap of panic at times, thinking, "Oh my God, now what?"

Probably the biggest learning was going to countries like Pakistan, Iran, Turkey, even Malaysia, but Pakistan especially when I stayed with people from the Servas[10] organization. When I got home, people would say, "Weren't you afraid?" "Weren't you scared?" It's hard to explain, but I felt like, wherever I went in those countries, the people I met, not only the Servas people, felt a responsibility to look after me. It really seemed as though they were genuinely concerned I was a woman alone on a bike and they were there to see I was safe.

---

[10]   Servas International tries to encourage world peace through volunteers in more than one hundred countries who open their homes to travelers.

One day, I traveled across the middle of Pakistan with a police escort. I was passed along from one police jurisdiction to another. I didn't ask for their protection. It just happened.

I went into places where no one spoke English and within fifteen or twenty minutes, someone would appear who spoke English. Those kinds of things make you realize the universe is providing for us.

I tell people the world isn't as dangerous as we think it is. We hear the news; we hear all these awful things. We don't hear about the ninety-nine percent of people who don't make the news, who are like you and me, the average person living in North America. When I was teaching adults for a while in Thailand, they asked me if it was safe to travel in the United States. When I came back from my travels and was living with my sister, I can remember sitting and watching the Edmonton news a couple of nights in a row. There was a shooting in north Edmonton, someone had been killed somewhere else, there was a knifing in south Edmonton close to where my sister lived — and I started to laugh. People asked me if it was dangerous to travel around the world? It's really an unfortunate perception because it keeps people from going places they would like to go, but they're afraid.

I loved some of the places I went in Argentina and Chile, beautiful little resorts where you could camp by the lake. I never for a moment felt in danger in South America.

People call me courageous all the time and I'm not. I have all the fears everybody has. I talk about this when I do some of my presentations, about how I had all these fears about not going. I've talked to so many women who have said they'd like to ride. Go take the course and then go from there. If you don't like it, you haven't lost anything.

A year after I had given a presentation on my trip in a small town in British Columbia, I returned to do a book signing. A retired lady came up to me. She said, "I finally did it. I took my first trip. I went to Germany by myself." That made it all worth while for me.

One of my fears before I left was that I was selling everything and using my hard-earned money to go and play. What was I going to do when I came home? But I developed this realization that things really do come to you when you need them. I needed a job, so I kept my eyes open and looked, but I didn't panic. When I did get a job, it paid more than I'd made in all my years of working other places.

Most importantly, my trip around the world was the biggest contributor to finding my self-confidence and self-esteem. It continues to grow.

Woody Woodward

Occupation: lover of life
Location: Boston, Massachusetts
Age: 64
Riding Discipline: street
Began Riding: 1971

Woody's energy and love of life is palpable as soon as you see and speak with her. She, too, has traveled the world.

She has spent her life following her heart, which has no limits. She has been a staunch activist and leader and contributed endlessly to her community. Often she led Boston's gay pride parade on her motorcycle, sporting her trademark brilliant rainbow Mohawk. In recognition of her tireless contribution to charitable causes, Boston Mayor Thomas M. Menino declared June 7, 2008, Woody Woodward Day.

I met Woody in person in Daytona during Bike Week. True to form, she had arranged her vacation around her chemotherapy treatments, flying down as soon as one was over, picking up a bike she had stowed with a friend in central Florida and riding it to Daytona Beach.

She didn't mince words about her treatment or prognosis, or the fact that she was living every moment to the fullest, as she had for her whole life anyway. Her hair was mostly gone, but I'll never forget her blue eyes, a perfect match to the Motor Maids ball cap she was wearing, sparkling with spirit.

I was always fascinated with wheels and with going somewhere. I loved motorcycles and wanted one desperately, but my parents were not at all motorcyclists and it was not an option then. But in 1971, I was in England working in archaeology and picked up a Vespa 150. When I came back to the States, I got a 305 SuperHawk Honda and that's when I really started being on the motorcycle more.

I had started traveling and living in Europe in November of 1966. I lived there for almost a year and then I came back for four months and then I went over again and I got into archaeology and did work assembling typewriters and as a chambermaid. In Australia I picked fruits and vegetables. Most of my life I've worked to support my motorcycling and traveling addictions.

I can still remember my grandmother when I first went to Europe in the 1960s. She was a very dignified older woman who had a hearing aid from the time we were little. She and her best friend said to me at one time, "God, you're so lucky, because we could never do that when we were your age." My father had never said, "No, you can't do that." Sometimes he would say, "It's not always easy, but go for it." I think he probably wanted to do all of the traveling, but he had to do it through my eyes because he had to stay home to earn the money to keep everybody in food.

Picking a favorite motorcycle experience is hard. I think about driving across the Australian desert from Perth over to Adelaide and experiencing the emptiness. Hardly anybody else was doing that in a car back in 1987, let alone on a motorcycle. The amazement of the Australian men when they would run into me on my motorcycle going across was evident. "Good on you, mate! Good on you, mate!"

When all of this virtual stuff came on the computer, somebody said to me, "No need to travel like you travel. You go on the computer and do a virtual tour." I said, "You'll never get stuck in the Andes taking a ride in a truck and being brought to the local manor, where all the locals bring all the stuff from the fields; where they're running a little restaurant, and have them come out and bring you in. You pay for a meal and they let you sleep on the tables that night. You teach them how to play crazy eights, you go in the kitchen in the morning, help the women peel the potatoes and then they find you a ride the next morning on a truck. You won't do that with virtual reality."

Four years ago, I was riding out to work at the Women's Music Festival in Michigan. I left on Sunday morning on my 1970 BMW and was making good time getting to New York City. I was cutting across Pennsylvania on a road that parallels the turnpike, heading for a friend's house in Ohio to spend the night. The bike stalled out and I couldn't get it started.

I called my friends and said, "I'll push the bike to the exit and you meet me there." So I was pushing and walking next to it, because I'm vertically challenged and can barely touch the ground when I'm on it. A van with a woman and two older guys stopped. They said, "Why don't you get in the van and take a rest and let us push it for a while?" They were very good. They pushed it to where I could meet my friends. I didn't have time to wait for parts, but I was able to keep the bike going with a charger for the battery.

I feel the most comfortable when I am in touch with my motorcycle and I can hear changes and sounds and I'm able to deal with something before it becomes an issue. That also reflects in my life, and that's one of the interesting things about being on the bike. The whole time I ride I'm paying attention and I'm really watching the road. I'm watching in front of me and to the sides and in the back, and behind with my mirrors. Mirrors are very important and some people don't remember to use them. They tell you where you've been. Being on a bike is also a time when you can work out things in your head. It's a very peaceful place. I like silence — I've never had a radio, music, even in my house. I can deal with silence and I can deal with listening to bikes. Knowing about your bike is empowering.

I have lots of bikes scattered around the country. I've got two on the road here in New Jersey; there's one down in Florida at a friend's house; and there's another Suzuki waiting to go on the road. I had another bike shipped out to Seattle a year ago last June because I was going to do a trip to Alaska, but then I was diagnosed with ovarian cancer and I couldn't go right away. We went this summer during a thirty-day period between my chemo treatments.

I volunteer on the local AIDS walk and I've been on the motorcycle safety crew for Jane Doe Walks. Since the inception of the

Pony Express Rides in 1996, I've participated in all of them. They've crisscrossed the country and raised over two million dollars toward cures for cancers.

I love when little girls and even little boys realize it's a woman on the motorcycle. I want them to see who's riding and I want them to know they can do it. My nieces and nephews are all used to it. The more people realize everybody can do everything, the more it excites me.

I have taken advantage of every moment. When I was diagnosed, the doctor, who wasn't very good anyway, said, "Oh, it's the bad-case scenario, not the good case." I got a little flippant. "That's all right. I've done pretty much everything as I've gone along, so I'm all right." "Don't you want to talk about it?" "No." "Well, I need to talk about it." "But I don't."

Woody passed away three months after I met her and just hours before the latest parade she had planned to participate in.

Lesley Gering

Occupation: mother, motorcyclist, journalist and artist
Location: Vancouver, British Columbia
Age: 38
Riding Discipline: street
Began Riding: 1981
Website: motorgirl.com

Lesley considers herself a mother first, but that's just the beginning. Her life is an eclectic combination of art, writing, photography, spirituality, motorcycling and technology. Her visceral artistic style exudes her vibrant spirit. This spirit has taken her on her motorcycle to the top of the Himalayas in Nepal and to Northern India and Eastern Europe as she explored the link between modern technology and ancient rites. As an award-winning Emily Carr artist, she combines media to create unique pieces, even incorporating sprockets and used motorcycle oil into her paintings.

She is also an accomplished writer and photographer, published in over a dozen magazines internationally. She has disassembled and put together more than her share of bikes. She is involved in a variety of activities aiming to encourage more women to get out there and ride.

Lesley connects with her spirit no matter where she is, but finds the best place to meditate is on her bike, especially in storms.

This year is the first year I've really been able to get back on the road properly after having babies, my marriage ending, being a single mom and so many other personal tragedies that seemed to be happening one after the other. One of my best friends died, I had another loss in the family, and I've had a really heavy load on my heart. Being back in the studio with my first big solo art show in a long time, I was sinking. I wasn't even moving any more. Artistically, I was stuck. I couldn't even feel my heart beating. I just knew the only medicine that would fix it would be to take off on my motorcycle.

The idea of leaving my children was so difficult, but I had to go. I took twenty-one days off and rode on an amazing journey. My main goal was to get to Burning Man[11].

I've been going since 1999, except for a hiatus when my babies were born. It's kind of insane to go by motorcycle. You need so much stuff, including all your water, at least six liters a day just to survive. Last year, out of fifty thousand people, only ten or so arrived on motorcycles. I had friends bring all my stuff down and I did this amazing journey where I was over the mountains, down in the deserts, across the rivers, through the gorges, over the mountains, along the ocean, up the coast, down the coast, through the forest fire, up over here — and then rode in to the plaza at Burning Man into a dust storm that took me two hours to get through. I had to pull myself in on my motorcycle along a fence line wearing a mask and goggles. I landed at my camp to raucous cheers and literally fell off my bike. It really felt like the winds had taken away all the anger and sadness from the year and I really felt good, like I was coming back into my power. Alive. I could feel my skin and I could feel my heart beating.

And then it was this beautiful, very spiritual week for me. I was bringing my friend's ashes there and I was fire dancing. Talk about being powerful. There's nothing like twelve hundred fire dancers dancing around this ten-story burning man and another five thousand drummers around as well. I came home totally inspired and completely rejuvenated and I felt like every part of my life was better for it. Motorcycling for me is that kind of medicine.

I'm struck when I see a woman rider who's being herself, just being who she is and expressing herself through riding. I'm always

---

[11] An annual one-week art event in Nevada's Black Rock Desert. A temporary community of up to 50,000 converges for radical self-expression and self-reliance.

impressed when I see a girl and they're riding really well and they're wearing all their gear and they're being safe and they're encouraging other women to do the same.

I started riding motorcycles in orchards in the Okanogan with my neighbor friends, because they had dirt bikes and I was not allowed to have one. I used to sneak over and ride through the trees with them. Later, I did the same thing when I was out with friends and they would get me bikes to ride. When I was in my early twenties, word got back to my stepfather that I was riding around on these big Harleys. He had a little chat with my mother and said, "She's going to do this. She's been doing this. Let's get her taking this course and getting some proper training. It sounds like she's actually a pretty good rider."

I never got off a motorcycle after that. I was riding all year round in Vancouver, all through my university years, and rode every kind of bike you can imagine. Usually my boyfriends or other friends knew about motorcycling and they taught me a lot. I listened and I took a lot of courses where I totally disassembled a motorcycle and put it back together. It was awesome.

While my sons were young, I made a conscious effort to keep motherhood and motorcycling separate. Several times when they were babies, I was able to get out for a long ride — once for a week. It was nerve-wracking because I was still in wife and baby mode but it was so good because I felt like myself again. It's good for my sons to be away from me for a while and for me to have that longer duration of riding. I come back a completely changed person and I'm a much better mother. I have to take care of myself, my needs, my passions, in order to be the best mother I can be.

I liken it to the instructions for using the oxygen mask in the airplane. Mothers are supposed to put the oxygen on themselves first, then their kids. It's a hard lesson to learn.

Motorcycling, drawing, dancing and doing something artistic all go together. I stopped riding in the city a long time ago because for me the whole thing is the journey. I like getting out of the city, into the mountains, and that's where I get my power from. Being away and being able to take all my leathers off and jump naked into any kind of water, waking up in the mornings and looking at a map and deciding if I'm going to go north, south, west or east. Nothing is more powerful than that, than making myself mistress of my own destiny.

The freedom of being on the bike forces you to work. There's no television, no music, no kids in the car — there's no anything. You're in your head but you're also really focused on what you need to focus on. You have a really strong awareness of your body and you have a really strong awareness of your environment. It's the epitome of yoga. I have a hard enough time sitting still, let alone meditating on the ground. I can meditate when I'm on my bike, especially when I'm in storms. That's when I start really breathing and being. You've got to get out of the city, but once you get going, that's when you get the road trip that's really making sense to you and why you're on it.

It shows in all my art. My latest work is Tantric philosophy, which is all about mixing old physics formulas, motorcycle parts (especially sprockets and carburetors), the ideas of speed and everything I love about motorcycling. Then I combine it with sketches inspired by the Kama Sutra and the Tantric temples in Nepal, bringing in this sensual, spiritual side and creating highly complex art that makes a statement of who I be. I've started painting with used motorcycle oil. Whenever you see a black part of my paint, that's been mixed with motorcycle oil.

One of my favorite memories is going into this mountain town. I was in heaven from a glorious ride and I must have looked blissed out. Two cute little old ladies dressed really fancy, with lace and parasols, were in this store and I walked into the back, wearing all my leathers, a little bustier top, my big necklaces, big hair, big teeth, lipstick, and smiling my face off. They said, "WOW — are you Xena, the princess warrior?" And I went, "Yeah, I'm Lesley the motorcycle princess." That feeling of yeeaaahhhh, of course I am. They were so sweet. I ended up going over to their house, sitting there under their little umbrellas and having a little tea, which turned into having a little shot of sherry. I was in town to meet my friends at the Rod and Gun Saloon. How much more of a dichotomy could you get?

That is who I be.

Barbara Wynd

Occupation: bed and breakfast co-owner
Location: Lion's Head, Ontario
Age: 47
Riding Discipline: street
Began Riding: 1990
Website: taylormade.bb-bruce.com

Barbara and I met cleaning cat cages as volunteers at the SPCA. She had just moved to Canada from Norway and was establishing a new life here, prior to purchasing the B&B with her now-husband. She used her motorcycle first to test her independence and then shipped it to Canada to begin a two-month, life-changing adventure at almost the same time as mine.

Growing up in Germany, I always wanted to ride, but my parents asked me not to and I was always a good girl, so I didn't. I did take every opportunity to ride on the back, though. My first husband had a bike and I spent two years as a passenger. I talked to him of course about wanting to ride and he always said yes, it's dangerous, but you can do that. So, when I was twenty-nine, I did.

I always wanted to ride alone, but he never let me. The only trips I got by myself were down to work and back on the Autobahn in Germany. That's not much of a trip and it's more stress than anything else.

But when we got divorced, I borrowed a little tent, I had my Harley and I said, okay this weekend is my first test weekend motorcycling by myself.

It was just one hundred and forty kilometers one way, but it could have been around the world for all the excitement I felt. Here I was doing my own thing and it was absolutely fantastic. I put up my tent in a spot where I was totally by myself and I enjoyed it. Nobody told me where I had to stop, what to eat, when to eat — it was just me.

I didn't think about anything, I didn't give it a deeper meaning or anything like that. I just wanted to try to ride alone. It was the start of a lot of trips by myself.

By this time, I was living in northern Norway. When I announced I was going on a two-month trip to North America to take part in Harley-Davidson's 100th anniversary celebration, everybody told me, "You are so brave." Brave? I'm not brave. I wanted to have a holiday and nobody else went with me. I would not stay back because I'm alone.

That trip changed my world. In the anniversary campground with approximately twelve thousand tents, fourteen thousand bikes and sixteen thousand people, I met some wonderful friends, including the love of my life. We spent a fabulous week together before we all had to go our individual ways. I rode south to Key West but it was anti-climactic and by the time I got there, I knew I had to visit him in Canada once more before I returned to Norway. I headed north to Orangeville for a wonderful week together before we shared a tearful good-bye and promised to see each other again.

Five months later, I was back in Canada with an eight-month visa, enough to test the relationship. After only a couple of months, we bought a B&B and settled in the beautiful Bruce Peninsula of Ontario, reminiscent of my home in Norway. The following summer, we flew to Las Vegas, rented a Harley and got married at the drive-through chapel.

Riding influenced my life in a major way because without it I wouldn't be here. I met people who I really liked. In Germany, everything is very strict, but when you're out on a motorbike and you meet another biker, you have something in common and you just talk. There is no barrier.

It also boosts your self-esteem. If the unexpected happens and you apply lots of brake, make the bike stand sideways and it is still upright, you say, I can do things I didn't think I could do. And that of course gives you confidence in other situations. I know I can do that and if there's anything else I would really like to do, I know I will be able to, because I did that with motorcycling, too. If I want something to happen, then I can make it happen.

I have a lot of fellow riders up on the Bruce Peninsula and these girls are fantastic. They are so vivid. They ride with the confidence of powerful women. They have this certain *je ne sais qua*. "Yeah sure, I'm riding a bike. So what?" They are all very interesting and have attained a certain level of achievement.

When I was taking the course in Canada, I saw a lot of women tried it because their husbands said they should. To them, I say, "Leave it. Don't do it for somebody else. Do it only for yourself."

If you do it and you really find your inner strength and you enjoy riding, it can give you back power. But if you just do it because he said to, and you still think you don't know how to ride, you're not where you're supposed to be. It is too dangerous. You have to be aware it can kill you, it can dismember you. You have to love it so much that you would be able to cope with that.

CHAPTER 9

Sharing the Legacy

"I love when little girls and even little boys realize it's a woman on the motorcycle. I want them to see who's riding and I want them to know they can do it, too."

—Lover of Life Woody Woodward

MY PARENTS ADORED THE "new" me and were thrilled to be part of the action. Our relationship became better than it had ever been. Although I live several hours away, the large barn on their property has been host to spring and fall motorcycle workshops I've held in their area. Dad would get the barn ready, clear out space, sweep the floor, set up chairs and lend me his tools. Both of them would join us for lunch and I don't know who enjoyed it more, my parents or the participants.

It was still hard to explain what I had always known. Trillium was more than a tour company. It was a way to get me started doing something I loved and the entry point into so many other opportunities that aligned with my goals. Tours were the core business activity, but I soon expanded into area day rides, women's only events, do-it-yourself motorcycle maintenance workshops, online classes, corporate events and focused networking rides. I sent out a monthly newsletter on current events, tips for riders and articles as well as the highlights of our rides. Early on, I began posting profiles on my website of riders I thought readers would find interesting: women and men with seemingly ordinary lives who were making a difference in their unique way.

I embraced my involvement with the Motorcyclists Confederation of Canada and its Women Riders Council. We were celebrating and promoting our sport and elevating its professionalism. We reached out to women in Canada but were able to build relationships with international partners while strengthening the confederation's ability to meet its goals for riders from all disciplines.

All of this work is voluntary, yet so vital for riders. Most of them are unaware so much energy is required to maintain the riding lifestyle they enjoy. While it's wonderful to go out and enjoy the ride and the freedom, most people are oblivious to the fact that freedoms are at risk. National and international decisions can affect our ability to make choices about such things as the types of motorcycles available to us, where and what we can ride and who we can take as passengers — to name a few.

Legislation infringing on motorcyclists' rights can be a bellwether for broader societal rights. For example, the introduction of a consistent method to measure sound emissions from vehicles makes sense. Targeting motorcycles only for sound level measurements does not.

Legislation can appear to affect only motorcyclists, but when you look at the bigger picture, much more is involved. When legislation is based on incomplete research and an irrational train of thoughts, and when it threatens to get passed before it's widely known, what other rights are at stake? Here again, it's not about the motorcycle; it's about the erosion of our rights and increasing accountability and involvement from the public beyond motorcyclists.

It came as an epiphany to me that, right from the start, I'd unknowingly set up resistance in my relationship with Hart. Granted, we lived in different worlds and faced challenges, but I hadn't realized

I was putting up my own barriers and expecting our relationship wouldn't work out. The insight gave me an even deeper appreciation of enjoying each moment, knowing all would work out as it was meant to. How could it then go wrong, no matter what the outcome? The whole idea of enjoying the present is to do just that and stop giving energy to things beyond my control and understanding.

Writing became my immediate priority — a perfect winter occupation for a motorcyclist. I continued with some part-time teaching I was committed to, but that was all. It was a leap of faith, because I had no other means of support. When the urge for paid work compelled me to interrupt my commitment to writing by scheduling meetings or events, something completely beyond my control would cause them to be rescheduled or cancelled. I finally stopped trying to interfere with what I was supposed to be doing.

The universe often sends me signs of encouragement that I'm on course. I can't know what's going on behind the scenes or what the lead up is, but when "coincidence" happens, it always amazes and energizes me. Motorcycles are usually involved, either directly or indirectly.

A case in point is how things came together for my involvement with the American Motorcyclist Association's International Women & Motorcycling Conference. The American association had invited its Canadian counterpart to become involved in the conference, which is held every three years or so. The Motorcyclists Confederation of Canada (MCC) saw this as a perfect opportunity to establish a closer working relationship with the U.S. group and increase the awareness of MCC nationally and abroad, which was vital for its ultimate effectiveness in Canada. Our Women Riders Council (WRC) was excited to be a part of this premier event and as WRC chairperson, I connected with Tigra Tsujikawa, the American association's marketing and special events manager. (Her story appeared in Chapter Seven.)

Tigra is based in California. When we learned we would both be in Daytona for Bike Week, we made plans to meet in person. The allure of Bike Week for me has less to do with going to Florida to ride my bike in March and more with spending a mid-winter break with friends. In fact, I didn't even take my bike down. Hart was with me and I was quite content to be a passenger for that week and be ferried around and feted in style.

It was wonderful to meet Tigra, and other members of the AMA team, and that meeting also led to an active, visible role for MCC in the conference. None of that would have happened were it not for motorcycles and the common cause, albeit for different reasons, that brought all of us to Daytona.

Most importantly for me, the conference elevated the professionalism of women in motorcycling. I was both humbled and honored to be a part of that. The momentum and seeds of change started at the conference had positive repercussions that will be felt for years to come.

It was beginning to be apparent I was doing what I had set out to do. By creating an environment in which I could thrive, I had done the same thing for others. Doors were opening where none had existed.

I had discovered the treasure and it didn't come from anyone or anything. It came from within and was there all along. I had learned about the personal rewards and the phenomenal experiences that are available to us if we push past our concerns. When we find something this precious, it's too good to keep to ourselves and we need to share it so that others can experience the same thing. As emissaries, we know that the major obstacles to riding, and in fact to most other challenges in life, are the ones we erect ourselves. It's a matter of using our power to get past fear rather than fighting it.

The women whose stories follow have discovered the treasures that emerge through riding and are compelled to pass them along to others. They are involved in teaching, charity and advocacy organizations, speaking out and defending our rights. In serving, these women have brought many more into the sport. This work is often undervalued or not noticed at all, but it helps preserve the rights and freedoms all riders enjoy and has a positive effect on others and their communities.

Sue Slate

Occupation: Kawasaki Motors Corp., USA — Riders of Kawasaki;
Motorcycle Safety Foundation instructor; national programs chair,
Women's Motorcyclist Foundation Inc.
Location: Le Roy, New York
Age: 62
Riding Discipline: street, dual-sport
Began Riding: 1965
Website: womensmotorcyclistfoundation.org

Sue Slate and her partner, Gin Shear, have been named motorcycling pioneers by the American Motorcyclist Association's Heritage Foundation. Sue and Gin founded the national Women's Motorcyclist Foundation (WMF) in 1984, starting with multi-day gatherings to enhance the riding, mechanical and touring skills of women.

I met Sue at Daytona, where she was serving with the Riders of Kawasaki. She's another quiet hero — with two-inch soles added to her riding shoes so she can reach the ground.

Since 1993, Sue and Gin's non-profit organization has been raising money to fight breast cancer through events like the Arctic Tour — Ride for Research; and Pony Express tours. The number of people who have been touched by her spirit without ever meeting her boggles the mind.

Sue emphasizes the importance role models have played in her life and in shaping who she is. Those role models would be proud to see their influence has grown exponentially through Sue and the living legacy she is creating.

My upbringing gave me a distinct advantage. My father was a home contractor and he did everything. He dug his own basements, he made his own cupboards and he installed his own septic systems. That meant he had a lot of equipment — a bulldozer, trucks, a tractor, plows and you name it. As I kid, I had an affinity for those things and loved to be outdoors, to go fishing, to go to work with my dad. I never really gave it a lot of thought. When I was a teenager trying out my buddy's dirt bikes, it never occurred to me this would be something difficult.

I got my first road bike when I was a freshman in college. I didn't have the money for my dream bike, so I wound up with a ninety dollar, ten-year-old Honda 150 Dream. It leaked oil and it was pretty bad, but for ninety dollars I got quite a bargain. I learned to take care of that bike. It was old enough that it was hard to get parts, so to seal oil leaks, I had to cut my own gaskets and do all kinds of things that built my confidence as a rider. Ultimately, I can look back at it as fortuitous that I was too broke to buy a dream bike.

My favorite trip was our first fundraiser, a partial road and dual-sport ride to the Arctic in 1993. That was pretty spectacular and it turned out to be life altering. It changed the direction of our lives, our work, our mission, everything.

Four of us had decided we were going to take a trip to the Arctic Ocean by motorcycle, through the Yukon and the Northwest Territories. As we were planning that trip, we learned of the statistics on breast cancer. We were agog over the fact that we all were ignorant of the facts: one hundred and eighty-eight thousand U.S. citizens were getting breast cancer and we were losing forty-seven thousand a year. We decided we were going to make this a fund-raising mission instead of a vacation.

It took us about a year and a half to plan the trip and to get the money raised, and we were out there for thirty-nine days and we did fifteen hundred miles of dirt roads. It was an incredible journey at so many levels, including emotionally and in terms of taking care of ourselves. We had no chase vehicle; we just went. We had first aid and CPR skills, we had mechanical skills, we had decent riding skills and we had good mounts, and we just assumed we could do it and we did it.

Anything like this is so doable. It just takes dreaming, planning, preparation and then going for it. That's how I view life. You don't just do it. You do it with some forethought and some planning and you manage risks. But you take risks — healthy risks, and that's what this trip validated for us. We were working on this mission for almost two years, fund raising, getting the right gear together, planning the trip, knowing what to expect and how to handle different situations. We thought it would be just a one-time fund-raising trip to help eradicate breast cancer and it wound up becoming a driving force in our lives that we've been pursuing since. None of us had fund-raising experience. Our original goal was to raise ten thousand dollars. We've raised about two and a quarter million dollars so far.

It's joyful in that it's all grassroots. It's all volunteers and none of us get paid. I think grassroots efforts are important in that we're down in the trenches interacting with our friends and family and neighbors and that's where change happens, right there. Collectively, the whole thing together raises consciousness.

I want people to see motorcycling as user friendly. It's a great community and almost any challenge can be accomplished if you're prepared to handle it. I like to look at the goal out there and say, okay, what pieces of the puzzle do I need to put in place in order to get there? Then do it, and then go. It prepares me for the surprises that will happen along the way and I'm not nearly so overwhelmed. I still want a few surprises, though, because that's part of the adventure.

We were quite capable of taking care of ourselves. We had one rider who went down pretty hard in the dirt and her ignition module popped right out of the bike. It was destroyed. We were able to hotwire around it and use the kick start. We put a blanket down, took her forks off, slammed them on a rock and straightened them. We had a flat tire along the way and we were able to take care of that. We had dirt in switches and we lost lights and we were able to clean those out. We anticipated what we would have to do to avoid problems, but there's no way we were going to avoid everything, so we took the right tools, and knew how to use them. This is so doable. It's not great, huge strength. It's just get ready and go.

Motorcycling demands everything from you. It demands your intellectual awareness, your physical conditioning and your decision making. That's where the empowerment comes from. You are totally and completely responsible for yourself. Motorcycling can teach you that, if I can do this, then I can rise to other challenges as well.

When you're out on solo rides, you meet a lot of people because you're accessible and approachable. When you get off a motorcycle at a diner, anywhere, for breakfast or lunch, people are going to come up to you. It taps into a lot of aspects of joyful and full living.

Riding also gives you a healthy respect for life. You cannot do it without recognizing risks are involved. It reminds us both of our strengths as an individual and our fragility, and I think that's why motorcyclists are so charitable. When you appreciate the risks, you understand how simultaneously you're both powerful and vulnerable. The juxtaposition is kind of interesting.

It certainly has brought out my leadership skills. Most of what I do is involved with motorcycling, but certainly I have become a public speaker as a result of it. I've written articles for magazines. It has tremendously enhanced my communication skills and my self-awareness. The fact that I've been able to interact with so many people around the country and in Canada allows me to learn from a lot of different cultures and look at a lot of things differently.

One of the most beautiful things, the most poignant things, about motorcycling is it's a common ground when you break bread together on a mission such as raising money for breast cancer. Then your differences become something to be viewed as beautiful rather than something to be fearful of. We've had great diversity in our rides and people who are rubbing elbows probably never would have met had they not become motorcyclists. That breaks down barriers as well. There's just so much motorcycling has done for me and the community of motorcyclists. I feel very blessed.

For me personally, it's grow or die. If I'm not moving forward, I'm just standing still and that is just existence. Motorcycling is about motion and life is about motion. It becomes a life habit to reach out, and the more you reach out, the more you grow. The more you grow, the more you reach out. It's pretty much a self-fulfilling reality. If you extend yourself, you learn, and then you bump into somebody who maybe needs your learning, and then you bump into someone else and they have something to share with you that you need to learn. It's natural, like learning to talk or learning to walk.

You'll always find challenges along the way, and success breeds success. It gives you the confidence to face the next challenge and to kind of develop a different perspective. Is this really the end of the world? Probably not. That perspective also comes from working on this mission for breast cancer and interacting with so many survivors.

I expect more from myself than I do from anyone else, and I recognize that, but I also like myself. Not too much ruffles me. I can usually take a step back and say, how do we get up, around or through this little obstacle? Tenacity is part of riding. You put up with all kinds of weather conditions and breakdowns. It's the stuff of stories for when you're sitting in a rocking chair someday.

Since we are a minority and since it is viewed as an adventurous avocation, I think that when women or girls see other women riding, it says to them that, well, maybe I don't want to ride a motorcycle, but maybe I'll try hang gliding or maybe I'll try flying lessons or maybe I'll be a politician or maybe someday I'll be President. It still sets the tone that you can do anything if you put your mind to it.

Stefy Bau

Occupation: owner, 211 MX School
Location: Tallahassee, Florida
Age: 34
Riding Discipline: motocross (MX)
Began: 1983
Website: 211MXSchool.com

Whether it's as a motocross racer or an international pioneer, Stefy Bau is used to being first. She has won fourteen Motocross Championships (Italian, U.S. and World). Last fall she spoke at the International Working Group on Women and Sport, a United Nations agency — the first time motorcycling was ever represented. To think this was the pinnacle of her career would be to underestimate her drive and determination.

Stefy and her partner, Julia Keates, founded 211 MX School in 2010, aiming to empower women in sports. Since then, Stefy has received invitations from around the world to hold schools in countries as diverse as Indonesia and Iceland.

One need only speak with her for a few minutes to catch the fire and her commitment to serve and empower other women.

I entered my first race when I was six. I told my mom and dad, "One day I will become the first woman to become professional in the United States." As a little six-year-old Italian girl! And I ended up doing just that. It was just a gift that was in me.

Riding came naturally to me. Both my mom and dad were motocross fans, although they never competed. From the time I was born, they would bring me to the races every season. At four, I asked if I could have a motorcycle. And they said yes. Of course, this was very different from the cultural belief of Italians. You don't have a little girl with a motorcycle. At least you didn't back then. I was expecting a toy, one with a battery in it. Instead my dad got me a Peewee, a real although very small motorcycle.

Geared up, I looked like a robot. They put me on the bike, said, "Okay, this is the field, this is the throttle and this is the brake. Go!" And immediately I knew how to ride.

Not long after, my dad was driving around and noticed a small motocross track buzzing with kids. He came home delighted. "Get dressed! We're going to a motocross track!" The other parents told my parents there were actually races for kids. My parents had no idea. Within an hour of being on the track, I was beating all the little boys.

That was when my adventures really started. We entered the first race that was close to home. I finished third, and from then on I won every race I entered, against all the little boys. I was the only little girl.

As I grew up and started making strides into the motocross world, I was considered by most a pioneer. There were very few strong championships for women, so I could not compete against other women. But I needed to show the world women can do this. My path was to try to compete against the men so I was at the same level as the men. In that way, you can inspire others. Eventually you get a full-on championship just for women.

By the time I was seventeen or eighteen, I could have competed alongside the men in the world championships. But Italy, being a conservative country, said, "No! We're not going to allow you to race against the men at the world level."

So I said, "Oh yes? Let me show you." I packed up everything, moved to the United States, started from scratch, became a professional and raced professionally in Supercross and Motocross against the men.

In 2003, organizers put on a race in Qatar for the best men in the world. Knowing I was at their level, I spoke with the promoter and asked if I could participate. The Middle Eastern culture is very different from Europe's or North America's. Having me participate was a big statement — and required me being surrounded by bodyguards at all times. CNN Arabia picked up the story and I ended up inspiring so many people.

Finally, in 2005, I was called to race the men's world championship in the round in Italy. That's the moment I'm most proud of, because originally I had had to leave my country to do this.

Then on October 25, 2005, the world as I knew it ended. I suffered a serious injury and could no longer race. I won't lie. I had some very difficult moments. You feel lost. You say, "Oh, my God, now what?" That was the toughest period of my whole life. Mostly it was the fact that I wasn't prepared. I was training for the upcoming season. Your mind is working at that point, visualizing you at the races, winning and on the podium. Then everything stopped.

Somehow I gathered myself together. I told myself, "Well, it probably happened in this way, now, so I can share my knowledge and my spirit in other sectors of motorcycling." And that's how I turned it around. A chapter of my life had closed and a new one opened up. I'm really happy with what followed. Riding a motorcycle had taught me since I was a little kid that you can overcome difficulties if you want to. I did it then with a big injury and I will continue to do so because it's a better way of living.

Motorcycle racing has taught me the spirit of sacrifice, the spirit of never give up, the spirit of collaborating, the spirit of always prove yourself and the spirit of honesty. Those are all things you transfer over to your regular life. So, when times get tough, I've learned to assess the situation, turn the negative into the positive and keep going. And this is how I have taken every single step of my life's adventure.

I feel privileged to be recognized in big venues for what I've done, and I will just keep going, to inspire others and show how maybe the little world of motorcycling does have a spot in the world in general.

Noora Naraghi is a prime example of how powerful motocross is as an agent for change. In defiance of Iran's cultural and legal system, she organized a women's motocross race last year at the MX club she and her family own. Then she came over here to my 211 MX school, and I taught her not only MX skills but also how to be a teacher for others. Now she is back in Iran, wanting to teach motocross to other women. The movement is growing.

Founding 211 MX in 2010 was a dream come true. We take students at our home base in Florida, but we also hold camps around the world. I'm somebody who was lucky enough to have a successful career in racing and after racing. I like to teach all my students that you can make a big plan out of this. Motocross as a sport may be short, but you can change your goal and keep going.

I believe I'm the first one to transfer successfully from the racing to a leadership position in the industry. And I think this is pretty inspiring as well. This is something I do teach at the school. What you can do one day becomes a way you can give back to your sport.

I love to be able to share what I've done with my life. It's like giving a little bit of myself directly to my world instead of just seeing the results on paper.

Gwen Roberts

Occupation: publisher, co-owner, Motorcycle Mojo Magazine
Location: Barrie, Ontario
Age: 50
Riding Discipline: street
Began Riding: 1988
Website: motorcyclemojo.com

Gwen had no idea when she married a biker that one day she'd be publishing a national motorcycle magazine. I've watched the magazine evolve from a small start-up to an acclaimed, widely read, national publication with articles of interest to men, women and even children.

Gwen, her husband and her daughter are all immersed in the sport and their family values are reflected in not only their product but in the generous contributions they make to the motorcycling community nationally through their participation in and sponsorship of events.

Following her heart and committing to serve riders has been inspirational for thousands of readers.

At thirty, I met a man with a motorcycle who would become my husband four years later. I had never been on a bike, although I always wanted to try it. I thought I was just marrying a guy with a motorcycle. I never dreamt I'd be getting into motorcycling as much as I have now.

He stopped riding when our daughter was born, but when she was two years old, he picked it up again. She was always interested in the bike, so I got my license, too. My first bike was a 250 Honda Rebel, which was great to start with, but I still wasn't sure I liked riding so I sold it and didn't ride for a couple more years.

When our daughter got older, though, she was always riding on the back of her dad's bike and I was following in the truck. I thought, we either have to get a sidecar or I have to get another bike. I saw a Buell Blast at a motorcycle show and had that for a year. I moved on to a Suzuki Volusia and then to the Harley-Davidson Softail Deluxe I have now.

My husband and I left for a weekend in New Brunswick one beautiful Friday morning at seven o'clock, each on our own bike. We enjoyed a wonderful weekend and left Sunday around noon to come home again. It poured rain the whole way back, almost like hurricane weather. We were heading into Quebec and the trees were blowing over sideways and we knew we had to get off the road. We just made it into the hotel as it came down in sheets. The storm sewers were overflowing and the parking lot had six inches of water.

People usually kind of panic when they drive in rain, but suddenly on that ride I felt so comfortable with it. We were passing transports on a two-lane road, so we had to pass them carefully, but it just didn't seem to bother me anymore. It was a frightening experience at first because I was being blown over and moved around a bit and was soaked and miserable, but it was a good thing to overcome my fear of riding in the rain. Now it doesn't bother me. When it first starts raining I kind of take it easy, and then after a while I'm okay with it.

The next day it was still pouring. We stopped at a restaurant and I wrung my socks out. They were just so soaked. Rather than put them on again, I decided to go without them. I thought my feet would be frozen, but they were just so hot I couldn't believe it. Maybe that's another lesson. If it's raining out, you don't need socks.

When something really bothers me while I'm riding, I need to pull over, take a break, regain my confidence and go again. That's all you can do. Shake off whatever scared you, whether it's something you did or another driver cut you off. You have to step back for a second until you feel good about going out again.

Overcoming challenges on the road has had other positive repercussions in my life. Some days you get overwhelmed with work and you just have to step back and do a little bit at a time. Things come more naturally the more you practice them and the longer you do them.

If you have a tough day at work and then head home at night on your motorcycle, you have a whole different feeling than if you're sitting in your car in traffic like everybody else. If you're on your bike, it's like you're in a different zone. You are on your own, you can go at your own pace and you can take a nice little side tour if you choose. It's a good stress reliever, especially if you're not in a rush to go anywhere. You can enjoy your surroundings.

Motorcyclists can talk to anybody about anything. If you see another motorcyclist, they're always open to talk with you, but if you're driving a car you wouldn't do that. It is a more open relationship with other bikers and with other people. You just have this connection, a kind of a warm, friendly feeling. It makes you a better person, because you take the time to talk to people. It helps you with people skills and with life in general, just because you're more aware of things.

When our daughter was ten, my husband had her on the back of his bike and we took our time riding all the way up through the Gaspé on our way to Cape Breton and New Brunswick. We were actually heading to Newfoundland, but by the time we got to Cape Breton, she had had enough of riding and just wanted to hang out with her cousins.

The whole trip was a wonderful family time. To keep our daughter entertained, my husband had on a backpack to which he had rigged a DVD player. People in cars were taking pictures of her, just sitting there on the back watching movies. We have wonderful memories of rolling down the road together, sitting around the campfire and heading to bed early so we could get up early in the morning and head out again.

She's sixteen now, and she doesn't want to go on the back with her dad anymore. She wants to ride her own bike, a 250 Ninja we picked up. She instructs in an off-road riding program and has had a lot of dirt-bike experience. She just needs to learn the rules of the road, and that takes a little bit of time to gain.

With our daughter on the road now, it's a whole new experience again. She was talking to her uncle in Cape Breton yesterday and told him she was going to ride her bike down this summer. Her plan for family trips now is she'll take her bike and we'll take ours. We have three people in the *Motorcycle Mojo Magazine* office now, so it will be easier for my husband and me to get out. With cell phones, computers and email, it shouldn't be that difficult to escape for a little bit.

I look forward to the years ahead when she's riding with us. That will be a fun family adventure time again. I'm hoping to get a few rides in on her bike and she's looking forward to riding mine. It's kind of neat to be exchanging things. Before we just exchanged shoes; now we can exchange motorcycles, too.

Yolanda Tesselaar

Occupation: sales analyst, senior motorcycle instructor
Location: Toronto, Ontario
Age: 42
Riding Discipline: street
Began: 1988

Yolanda and I teach in the same motorcycle program. She has an ability to boil down the lesson and present it in such a manner that the salient points are covered concisely and the students meet their objectives. She has a quiet, assured manner both on and off the course.

Yolanda is a single mom, raising her son and her teenage niece. Motorcycling has played a significant role in giving her the confidence she projects today. She regards that role so highly she felt compelled to become an instructor, and over her eighteen years of teaching has influenced thousands of students. She will be sharing that same legacy with her family.

I always had a very strong sense of who I was. When I was four or five, I was at the babysitter's with my brother. He's two years younger than I am so I was very protective of him. I don't remember what it was, but the babysitter did something that made me mad. I wasn't going to put up with whatever it was so I took my brother by the hand and walked out of the house and down the street, confident I knew the way home. She came running down the street after us and brought us back, but I remember very clearly at that moment thinking, I'm not going to put up with this. From that moment, I have always had the confidence to know I didn't have to do what other people wanted.

I have always liked bikes, but as a female twenty years ago, it wasn't really something women did. I was dating someone who had a motorcycle, and like most other women, I was riding on the back.

Then I met a woman who had a motorcycle of her own. I thought, "I can do this. I don't need to be on the back!"

When I make up my mind about something, it just goes. I signed up for the course, got a bike, passed the test and started riding. It all happened within four months.

Meeting people and traveling with them has been great. You have to have support as well, because if you're doing it on your own, it's really hard being a woman in the sport. But most people now have come to realize it's acceptable.

Early in my riding, I misjudged the distance to the stop at the end of a gravel road. I had a choice between braking really hard and going down on gravel or braking enough to slow down and then going into the ditch. I decided to go into the ditch. Try as I might, I couldn't get my bike out, because it had been raining and was quite muddy. A lady came along walking her dog, and it turned out she had a motorcycle in her past. She put burlap on the mud so the back tire would catch. That was tough, because I was out there by myself, but help appeared when it was needed.

For years after that, I was terrified of being on gravel. It really shook my confidence and I had to resolve that. Even today, I'd have to say it's still stayed with me, but I do it.

Riding has been a hugely rewarding experience, and teaching others to ride is right up there. You start the course and all these people, often older and mostly men, rely on you to teach something they have no idea about. It builds more confidence in you. And it translates into other parts of your life. You're not afraid to stand up in front of a group and tell them what you know without feeling maybe they're going to laugh at you.

Two summers ago, my twelve-year-old niece came to visit and liked it so much she decided to stay. We made all the arrangements with her parents and she's been living here with me ever since.

Deciding to leave a relationship and then have a child on my own as well was not something I thought of as hard, although I know it won't be easy. This is what I want, and if I don't get this, then my life is not going to be going in the direction I want to go. I approached it the same way as I approached learning to ride or other challenges. I really try and judge where I'm going before I make a mistake, and it rarely happens that I misjudge anything. But if I do, I try to focus more on recovering rather than just letting things happen.

I could have stayed in that relationship, but I knew I wouldn't have a child, or if I did, it would just be a complete disaster. For me, having a child on my own is more appealing than having a child with someone who is on a different path than I am and then having to deal with that person forever.

It's still hard for women to get into motorcycling. I see it every time they come to the course; you can already tell which women are probably going to make it and which ones are going to struggle. If they're lacking confidence or coming into the course with the idea that they shouldn't be riding, they'll have trouble with it. As a woman instructor, sometimes we have to give some of our confidence to these women. Sometimes they can get through it and sometimes they can't.

I'm always surprised when people say I'm courageous, because for me it always seems as though whatever I'm doing, whether it's riding or raising a child on my own, is something I'm supposed to be doing.

CHAPTER 10

Riding Your Own Ride

"Motorcycling teaches you to listen to your inner voice,
because it could be a life or death situation."

—Journalist/Entrepreneur Genevieve Schmitt

I KNEW AUGUST WAS GOING TO be a transition period. A subtle but definite scent of change was in the air that I knew would enable me to serve my purpose more effectively. What that would actually look like and how it would unfold for my business or my personal life I didn't know. I was stepping into the unknown again. But then, aren't we always? We just fool ourselves when we think all will work out according to carefully laid plans.

I was riding high after the success of the conference. Being involved in such a premier event was exhilarating and I had discovered personal attributes I didn't know existed. Here I was taking a leadership role for our Canadian contingent, hosting and riding with a former federal politician and meeting all kinds of amazing women — and men — who were making a difference in the lives of others. This book was well under way. Hart and our motorcycles were together for a couple of weeks that month and I knew from experience he was always there to accompany me through major transition periods. What else was I capable of and what lay ahead?

I had finally realized my heart is not in the tourism business per se; it's in the "personal growth through motorcycling" business. So, my business is changing as I hone my personal awareness. The calendar has more workshops and special events, and the orientation of the rides is different. All of the activities are designed to increase self-awareness, connect with others and perpetuate an environment leading to empowerment.

I was hanging on to one last bit of income security by continuing to teach business courses. But giving them energy closed the door to other opportunities that were aligned with my vision. I had to let go, not an easy thing to do when nothing else is on the radar. The last step was to let my Professional Human Resources designation expire. I didn't need it where I was going.

As I was preparing my own stories, and reviewing my journal entries from a few years ago, particularly from the crazy times of 2005, I laughed to myself. There I was, full of angst and worry about things that seemed so traumatic at the time. Now, though, I could barely remember the people I let get under my skin. I had a few more advanced lessons after that tumultuous year, but I was able to recognize incongruent motives more quickly and cut those characters loose when I could see we had different trajectories, although it's not always easy.

Motorcycling was in my life as my power animal relatively early, yet it didn't prevent me from steering off course. It was not until my Spirit came to the rescue that I began to learn about the power of the machine and my own personal power. Except for the core values, family and special friends that have remained constant, I would think that person in my younger body was someone else entirely. My "before life" is almost surreal. When I look back, I wonder who that scared, listless person was behind all those layers.

If I had not gone through that, however, I would not be able to appreciate the vibrancy of my life now. I had to step outside my comfort zone to get going through, and fortunately, I had a motorcycle to ease the way. As momentum picked up, all I needed to do was to shift into a higher gear and my bike was happy to respond.

Life is radically different. How could it not be after going through a tectonic shift? Almost all of the significant people in my life have appeared in the last eight years and not surprisingly, most are related to motorcycling. I could not have written this book any sooner.

I was talking recently with a close friend's sister, who remembered stories about my world travels and Yukon whitewater-canoeing expeditions. "You're the adventurer," she remarked. I smiled quietly. She was right. I had done things many people only dream of. But the real adventure has been becoming me and embracing who I am. The real adventure is part of every day.

My preoccupation with financial security has subsided, but certainly not as a reflection of my bank balance. I've learned I can have all the money in the world and if the universe decides to take it, nothing I can do will stop that. It really boils down to having the confidence to know what I'm doing is the right thing for me to be doing. It's reassuring to remember the same power that is in me also moves the planets in their orbits around the sun. Financial and physical security are illusions, and certainly are not where my strength comes from. As they cease to have control, I can get the real work done: making a positive difference in the world and creating that environment in which others, too, can push their own limits and thrive.

Meanwhile, Hart and I recognized sadly it was time to go our separate ways for good. We both viewed the relationship we had shared as a precious gift for the time we had it.

I don't know what is down the road but I am confident I'm on the right path. My life is richer and fuller than it has ever been and that spiritual bank balance keeps growing every day with a rate of return unheard of in traditional banks.

When I get on my motorcycle now, I don't think "what if." I get on and ride. Of course I know there are dangers but I have prepared myself as much as possible, watch for them while I'm out there and have the skills to respond appropriately. I change the oil and inspect my bike regularly for any changes. I check that the chain tension and tire pressure are correct and the tires are in good shape. I don't understand all the mechanical, technical and electrical complexities of my bike. I do know, however, that if I pay attention to it, perform routine maintenance, replace worn parts and tend to its needs, it will serve me well. I don't understand everything that happens in my life, but I do my part to keep myself physically, emotionally and spiritually healthy.

I make sure that if I'm fatigued or not feeling well, I don't ride. I know it is my hand that controls the throttle and the brakes, and I don't let anyone else pressure me into riding in a manner I'm not comfortable with. Too much is at stake.

There is peer pressure to ride our bikes to work when we're instructing, supposedly as a motivator for students. "Riders Ride," I hear. I know, however, that at the end of a summer day, when I've been out for nine hours in the hot sun on the pavement, I'm fatigued and it's not safe for me to be operating a motorcycle. I take my car on those days and ignore the comments.

When I'm not leading tours, I prefer to ride alone or with one or two other select riders whose skills I'm confident of and familiar with. On rare occasions, I ride with a group socially, but if they are riding more quickly than I choose to go, I hold back. Not so long ago, my riding was riskier than it is now. My bike and I are still capable of fast sport riding, and it's exhilarating, but it belongs in a controlled environment, not on the street. Aside from being dangerous, you're so focused on technical skills, you can't appreciate the experience you're traveling through. If others want to ride faster, I'll meet them there.

I make myself as conspicuous as possible and always wear full coverage, good quality riding gear, including a full face helmet. I value my face too much and have spent too much on dental work not to. It can be hot and bothersome but I'm worth it.

I know my bike has all the power I will need and all I have to do to steer out of sticky situations is call on that power. It has been with me through all of my most valuable lessons. We have learned a lot together and it knows me and what I need, better than anyone. I'm sure we have a lot more lessons to learn.

My motorcycle is a part of who I am but it does not define me. When I'm riding, we're one. But if it was taken from me, my spirit would still be the same. I'm convinced our motorcycles, especially aptly named Triumphs, are the earthly versions of unicorns depicted transporting angels around the heavens.

If we were able to look back at ourselves from outer space, way beyond our galaxy, the things that cause us sleepless nights, like finances, how someone treated us or whether we've made the right career choice, are minuscule in the grand scheme of things. When we discover the things that are important to us, our families, communities and the world we live in, that's what we focus on and that's how we make a difference. Just like when we ride our motorcycles, we keep our eyes focused on where we're going, looking as far ahead as possible and keeping a steady hand on the throttle. We see and acknowledge the obstacles we once feared but we know how to get around them skillfully and not have them detract from our journey.

Each person who comes into my life is a teacher with a special timely message. I used to think other people's opinions mattered more and were better than mine. It's taken a while to realize they are seeing the situation through their own eyes, filtered by their experiences, thoughts and beliefs and projecting their own thoughts on to my situation. Now I listen, respect their values, aspirations and good intentions, thank them and follow my own inner guidance. None of us can walk in another's shoes, so no one knows what's right for me other than me. As long as I stay centered and grounded, I will do just fine.

Rediscovering that power that resides within each of us and connects us to the universe puts everything in perspective. We can view our lives as observers, knowing extraneous events, like economies, conflicts and the need for the latest gadget, cannot have power over us. Sure, they affect the world we live in, but they arise out of the demands of our egos and their effects are no match for our spirits — unless we allow them to be.

We are riding our own rides. We've developed and honed our instinctual skills, connected with our wild nature and now embrace it. We love who we are and embody empowerment and joyful and full living in all aspects of our life. We are change agents and leaders, often in subtle, unplanned ways and without even being aware of it. We're closer than ever to who we are. We know our power is there and how to use it appropriately. All we have to do is call on it.

These pioneers and role models have all excelled and advanced to positions of leadership in vocations including business, politics and motorcycling. To a one, they are so humble and grateful for the abundance in their lives. They have all risen to the top in fields not traditionally populated by women, yet these women have not viewed their femaleness as an obstacle to success.

They set goals and steadfastly go after them, guided by their own intuition. They have not been held back by self-limiting thoughts and beliefs. When they've experienced setbacks, they haven't even considered what some of us would throw up as barriers. They've persevered with determination, persistence and tapping into their own power.

Leslie Porterfield

Occupation: Owner, High Five Cycles
Location: Dallas, Texas
Age: 35
Riding Discipline: street, racer
Began: 1992
Website: leslieporterfield.com; highfivecycles.com

I met Leslie at the AMA (American Motorcyclists Association) International Women Riders Conference in 2009. This amazing woman already held three land-speed records on the Bonneville Salt Flats, was the first female racer to belong to the Bonneville 200 miles per hour club on a conventional motorcycle and had been named the 2008 AMA Racing Female Rider of the year. The same year she was awarded the Bonneville Women's Spirit Award. Her two-way average of 232.523 mph got her into the Guinness World Records for the fastest speed reached on a conventional motorcycle by a female.

In 2009, she became the first woman to take the Top Speed of the Meet award on a motorcycle with her 240 mph pass against a record of 227 mph. She followed that with a Top Speed of the Meet on a Motorcycle Award at the BUB Speed Trials.

Leslie is also a national spokesperson for the charity Stand Up For Kids.

I got into motorcycling on a whim. Little did I know it would encompass my life the way it has. The motorcycling community has become my surrogate family. It's how I've met most of my friends and now it's my livelihood as well. I have a motorcycle dealership. I attribute my success in business and life to my passion for motorcycling.

At sixteen, I needed cheap transportation. My neighbor had a 1,000 cc cruiser in pieces in his garage, which he sold to me for two hundred dollars. I didn't know anybody who rode and had never been on a motorcycle but it seemed like a good, inexpensive mode of transportation. I decided I could manage to get that basket of parts running. People scoffed at me. Everybody said I'd never be able to ride it. Everybody said I'd never get it running. And that just made me, a scrawny, extremely shy teenager, more determined to do both things. Motorcycling brought me out of my shell and changed my life forever.

I've had the same reaction with the nontraditional approach I've taken in businesses. Construction, building houses and now the motorcycle dealership are definitely male-dominated fields but I never thought I couldn't do them. Others said, "Really? That's ridiculous! You'll never be able to do that." I heard the same things at sixteen. I did it then, I've done it every time since and I will continue to achieve my goals.

My second bike, a CBR 600, got me hooked on the sport bike's handling, brakes, acceleration — and speed. At nineteen, a friend encouraged me to get my road racing license, so I went to school, tasted racing and absolutely loved it. I had found my niche.

The first time I went out to the Bonneville salt flats in 2007, I came off the bike at a little over one hundred miles an hour, broke seven ribs, punctured a lung and had a concussion. More worrisome to me than the big physical setback was the concern that I wouldn't be able to achieve my goals, that I might be banned from racing or that I might lose respect or support from other racers. When I got out of the hospital and back to town, I was so surprised at the outpouring of support. People would come into the shop having seen the footage on the Discovery Channel and say, "I can't believe you keep riding. I could never touch a motorcycle again." That thought never crossed my mind. I knew I would get back out there, go after my goals, not let it hold me back or be the excuse for me to quit riding or even change my life.

The first time back on the salt I put the wreck out of my mind. I focused on exactly what I needed to do with the bike to succeed and what I needed to do as a rider to make the perfect run. And I went out there after my big wreck and made history.

I deal with fear by staying calm and focused. I know I take risks in racing and I know things can happen. I got into a one hundred and ninety-four mile an hour tank slapper[12] at Bonneville this past year that lasted for almost a mile. I kept my focus, continued to fight it and finally got it back under control. Learning to master fear and not letting panic set in is a must for survival. At those speeds and even on the street during my commute to work, I've had scary moments when being defensive and keeping my head has saved my life.

Racing at Bonneville and also just daily riding has taught me patience. I've always been very headstrong and very aggressive when going after my goals. Knowing when to push the limits, when the time is right, when to say, "not now" or when to go full throttle are all lessons I've learned through riding. It can be very humbling at times, too — like crashing, but then getting back up and going back and defeating my record. That translates to so much in my life, because there have been times in business and my personal life where I've fallen and had to start from scratch.

Motorcycling is a completely different business than, say, a car business. You can drive a car every day and not have a passion for it. But the people who ride and enjoy motorcycles are just like me. They do it because they have a passion for it. They enjoy the freedom. Understanding that and understanding that people who come in the door of my shop are driven by that and not just the need for transportation makes a big difference. It's definitely taught me a lot about the people who ride and it's a really neat community.

The motorcycle industry has been hit extremely hard in the past few years. Many of my friends and competitors have gone out of business and I've struggled to keep my doors open. Not giving up, saying,

---

[12] A condition where the handlebars swing from side to side with increasing ferocity, also known as a speed wobble

"I'm still here and I can make this work," fighting against those odds, building it back up, trying new avenues and different directions is a lot like riding motorcycles. It's a lot like racing, too.

Riding has brought out a lot of my personal strengths. Some of them have been through the school of hard knocks in my youth. I crashed sometimes, and I learned. I had to pick up my bike, fix it and go on. Knowing nobody would come and take care of that little me has made me even more independent and confident. The freedom I experience with motorcycling and the empowerment I get from riding translates into my personal life as well.

That scrawny, almost fatally shy teenager has overcome the fear she was plagued with for so many years and now speaks to huge crowds. I was mortified the first time my agent booked me for a public presentation. Now I do so much of it and I enjoy it, especially because I talk about motorcycles. It comes naturally and I enjoy sharing my stories.

I don't look at what everybody else does and I don't look at what can't be done or what people expect. I set my sights and go for it. I don't see the same limitations people say I have, being a woman in racing or anything else. I've got the same things to work with as everyone else. I knew I could get out there and be competitive. A lot of people called me crazy for going out to Bonneville with a ridiculously fast machine that had never been run before at the speeds I've taken it. It was my dream, I knew I could do it and I did it. And that's how I live my life.

Deb Grey

Occupation: speaker, author, former Member of Parliament, awarded the Order of Canada for Public Service
Location: Qualicum Beach, British Columbia
Age: 57
Riding Discipline: street
Began Riding: 1968
Website: debgrey.com

Deb's book Never Retreat, Never Explain, Never Apologize *sums up her approach to life.*

She made Canadian history by becoming the first Member of Parliament (MP) for the newly created Reform Party and was then instrumental in those elected seats growing from one in 1989 to sixty in 1997, when her party became the Official Opposition in Parliament.

She got her motorcycle license as soon as she turned sixteen and has not been without a bike since. The jacket of her book has three photos of her, including one against a backdrop of the Canadian Parliament Buildings. All feature a motorcycle, effectively summing up its role in her life.

I've always been impressed by her strength of character, powerful presence, no-nonsense approach, adherence to her own personal values and humor. Her life of service has included giving back to the motorcycle community, often lending her name to charitable causes. She has navigated by her own compass from an early age.

At age thirteen, my sister's boyfriend took me for my first ride on the back of his Harley-Davidson and I knew immediately I would be a biker forever. He figured the best way to get through to the older sister was to have the younger sister lobbying on his behalf. That didn't work, but I was hooked on riding. My birthday is on July 1st, a national holiday, and when I turned sixteen, I was really upset I had to wait an extra day to get my license. Dad wasn't around and money was scarce, so we were all trained that we got jobs as soon as we could. I got this job at a little bakery and saved up enough money to buy a little Honda 150 and I loved it.

I'm a child of the Sixties. Everyone was doing dope and drugs and rock 'n' roll and making love on the beaches down in Stanley Park right in front of everybody. Mom thought, if Deb's going to be motorcycling, it's not that bad. She knew I was safe and responsible and paid for it myself.

When I started riding, women riders were a lot rarer than they are now. Everybody looked at you like you were from another planet. I never thought to myself, "Well, I'll show you and prove it to you." I thought, like the title of my book — *Never Retreat, Never Explain, Never Apologize* — get the thing done and let them howl. And that is how I've lived my life. I don't make a conscious decision to say I'm going to do it. I do it.

I had a 1982 Honda 900CB Custom when I made Canadian history on March 13, 1989, becoming the first Reform MP. During the 1997 election campaign that led to the Reform Party becoming the Official Opposition with Preston Manning as its leader, Preston flew into the Edmonton airport for a huge "hangar rally." I met him on my motorcycle and gave him a ride for the short distance from the plane to the hangar, all filmed by the national media. He's actually a great horseman but was really scared on the bike that day and I say I still have his claw marks in my back. We created quite a ruckus because we didn't wear helmets (we were on private property) but it sure gave us a lot of coverage. The Royal Alberta Museum contacted me recently because they are doing a Deborah Grey exhibit. I tracked that bike down and I have just donated it to the museum. That old bike is alive and well and I'm just as happy as a clam.

Motorcycling is magical. It clears your head and your spirit and allows you to think. It gives you quiet time, it gives you peace and you know you're in tune with nature when you're out there. There's that feeling of oneness with God. Because I've been riding for so long, that has always been my safe place to go and be. Nobody can phone you, nobody can bug you; you're just there. It's me, the road, the smells and God. It gives you complete clarity and allows you to put it together and say okay, let's think this through.

I don't really think about power. I never feel like I'm trying to prove anything by being on my bike, but I also know instinctively that if I'm behind an idiot, I don't have to worry much about him because I can pass him and get rid of him. But I don't think, "I'm a woman and I have power here and I can use it." No, I just think "what a jerk" and I pass. Leave him or her in the dust.

I always measure everything in terms of when I'm sitting in the old folks' home, when I can't ride anymore, I maybe can't see anymore or talk, who knows what shape I'll be in — I could be dead tomorrow. I could get smucked on a bike. But I know this — that I'll never have any regrets. And so I won't be one of those people who says, "Gee, I wish I had learned to ride a motorcycle," or do whatever.

My mother is an amazing woman and just before she turned seventy, something twigged that she was terrified of sky diving, and I can certainly understand why. But she decided this was a fear she needed to conquer. My mom, who could never even ride a bicycle, went and jumped out of an airplane and we were stunned. I, who had spent most of my life on an airplane, said, "Mom, why would anyone jump out of a perfectly serviceable aircraft?" And she just said, "Because I needed to do it. I did it and I'm *never* doing it again." She had that gutsiness where you say, "*Good on you!*"

That's the kind of stuff I *love*. Some people say, "I would love to ride a motorcycle." They tell me all about it and I'll spend a few moments chatting with them. But don't tell me you can't do it for this reason or you think you're too old or this or that. I can't be critical, because everyone has their own life to live, and I do understand there are exigencies that make it difficult for people. But if it's just a matter that you're going to talk, talk, talk about it, stop talking and go live. *Do* it. You don't want to live with regrets.

I have lent my name for the last few years to the Ride for Sight, where hundreds of motorcycles congregate in Olds, Alberta. We were ready for the banquet and I ran into some people I knew from way back when I taught school up in Dewberry. We had a great old visit, I'd finished my supper and everyone was just hanging around. My friends were thrilled about my motorcycle, so I said why don't I take you for a ride? I took each of the two kids for a little run out of town and then came back and their mom wanted to go, so I took her, too. It was just great and we had a wonderful time — one of those magical moments. As I returned, someone came running out. "Deb, where have you been?" "My old friends were here and I was riding." Apparently they were doing presentations in the hall, which I knew nothing about. They had called my name and called me up for a special award as honorary chairman and where was I? I was out riding.

That story probably exemplifies me.

My whole life philosophy is that we become more of what we are, and when I'm speaking, I talk about that so much. Go to the old folks' home and find the miserable old cranks who are there, squawking about the food, the nurses who never come on time and nothing is ever good enough. Guess what they were like when they were twenty-five? You know exactly what they were like. To me, that's a travesty. We become more of what we are, so you better think about who you want to be or who you don't want to be a little later on so you can do something about it now.

I'm going riding.

Audrey Alexandre

Occupation: retired
Location: Welland, Ontario
Age: 78
Riding Discipline: street
Began Riding: 1947

Pioneer Audrey is a quiet role model for Canadian women. She has paved the way to the benefits many enjoy today, making a difference not only for women riders, but in her community and among her friends and acquaintances. She started riding more than sixty years ago and rode continuously until she decided to stop in 2003. I had the pleasure of being welcomed into her home in Welland and the honor of presenting her award when she became the first woman inducted into the Canadian Motorcycling Hall of Fame. She's humble and casual about her accomplishments, as if they're nothing unusual.

Audrey's memorabilia fills her home, and in particular the Motorcycle Room. It's not often you walk into an almost eighty-year-old woman's home filled with motorcycle memorabilia.

Most prevalent are the Motor Maid awards: hospitality award, 1981; Golden Life Member for fifty years in the group, 1999; and gold ribbons for all the conventions she attended after her fifty-year anniversary with the group. Kingston in 2006 was the last one, and she had to travel by car.

She also has recognition as the World's Greatest Hostess for the Bob Harper Memorial; a plaque with "Congratulations on fifty years of riding from Harley-Davidson"; and all kinds of Harley memorabilia. She has displayed many photographs of herself with her motorcycle, including one of her as a young girl taking a friend for a ride in her sidecar. A needlepoint gift hangs on the wall, reading "Wind Beneath my Wings," the phrase painted on her last motorcycle.

She organized, planned and executed countless rides, rallies and conventions, and her sphere of influence is wide, but she prefers to be in the back row of photos, speaks humbly about her accomplishments and rolls her eyes when complimented.

My father had a bike and a sidecar when I was young, in the early 1930s. Even before I went to school, he'd take me in the sidecar or sit me on the tank in front of him and I got hooked. I decided in high school I wanted a bike, so eventually I got one. My dad thought it was wonderful. My mother was quite angry. My friends were all waiting for me to get good enough so I could take them for a ride. From then on, except for six months when my Harley-Davidson was stolen, I always had one until 2003, when I parked it.

The freedom got me hooked. The wind is in your face and away you go. My first bike was from the Canadian Army, a 1942, 45 cubic inch Harley. Sometimes I had difficulty keeping up with the guys on the bigger bikes because it was shaking up my insides so bad. My last bike was a '93 turquoise Heritage and I had "the wind beneath my wings" airbrushed on.

I was busy riding and didn't get married until I was thirty. I had two kids and I couldn't get out as much for a while there. As soon as they were old enough to be looked after and taken care of I was on the go again. My husband was also a rider but when we got married, he stopped. My sons picked it up, but not until I stopped. I think they were afraid I'd show them up.

I remember seldom being treated differently as a woman riding a motorcycle. In fact, the only time I can think of is when I stopped for gas during a rain. The guy hadn't wanted to come out in the rain to pump my gas and he dumped the gas all over me from the waist down.

One time I was going to Louisiana and somebody — I guess he caught up to me or I caught up to him — decided he was going to ride with me, but I'm sure he had a problem in his head. I think he had probably been in the army and been injured. I was scared that night to stay in a motel by myself. But I jammed the door shut good. I think that's the only time I got nervous. Sometimes I got onto roads I'd rather not be on but I got through it.

I was the first Canadian to join the Motor Maids, the oldest organization for women riders. A little magazine came out called *The Enthusiast,* which was a Harley thing, and you could send away this coupon and they'd send you a Harley magazine. The Motor Maids almost always had an article about what they'd been doing and I thought, I've got to get in touch with them so I can do it, too. They've always traveled all over and that intrigued me. In 1955, I was honored to become the Canadian national director.

I was pretty proud of myself for riding with a friend through California to a Motor Maids convention in 1986 in Yakima, Washington. I attended more than nineteen in all but that one stands out as a special trip.

I was the only female to become a member of a local motorcycle club when it was founded. They let me in at their second meeting, I think because they wanted someone to take the minutes. They've always been very nice to me and allowed me to use the clubhouse to celebrate my fiftieth year of riding in 1996, which was also their fiftieth anniversary.

I think I could still get on a bike, but it would be a job — on a Harley, anyway, because it leans so well.

My only advice to new riders is to make sure you get a bike that fits you.

When I see another woman rider now, I don't think anything other than she's having a good time, too.

Genevieve Schmitt

Occupation: founder/editor of Women Riders Now (WRN) and Trike Riders Now (TRN); leading spokesperson on women and motorcycling
Location: Livingston, Montana
Age: 44
Riding Discipline: street
Began Riding: 1990
Websites: womenridersnow.com, trikeridersnow.com, genevieveschmitt.com

Genevieve is a driving force in educating the industry and getting its attention for the fastest growing segment of motorcycling. She has facilitated the entry of many women into the sport through her tireless efforts.

Shortly after she began riding, she became a freelance motorcycle journalist, covering all aspects of and people in the industry. In 2000, she founded the award-winning Woman Rider *magazine. Her journalism won her induction into the Sturgis Motorcycle Museum & Hall of Fame in Sturgis, South Dakota, in 2001.*

In October 2005, she started Women Riders Now™, a marketing and consulting company. The website's online magazine is the leading source of news and information for women riders and those who are interested in the women motorcyclists' market.

She is often called upon by media and television shows to offer her expert opinion. She is compassionate, approachable, enlightened and driven. Genevieve embodies personal power and rides her own ride, whether it's on or off a motorcycle.

I was asked to create a segment on career women riding motorcycles when I was a producer on *Good Morning America* in 1990. I had nothing to do with bikes before then and didn't know any riders.

I rounded up fifteen women at this one location for the shoot, and it really struck me — not only were they all beautiful, but there was an energy around the women that I wanted be a part of. Even today, when I'm around a group of women riders, I feel that energy and that spirit among them.

Little did I know this moment would literally define my career path later in life. When I took up motorcycling in 1990 it gave me a renewed sense of confidence about myself. I certainly had confidence in my career, but when I was learning to become a rider — being able to handle the machine and handle the challenges of the road on the bike — it boosted confidence in other areas of my life. Motorcycling set me apart, and that was kind of cool when I was in my twenties, when we're all seeking some kind of identity.

The thing that impresses me most when I see a woman rider now is the fact that she's overcome mental challenges to get on the bike. I believe the majority of women riding today have had to wrestle with some self-imposed mental obstacle and/or societal stereotypes to give themselves permission to take up motorcycling. The other women have grown up around motorcycling; it was okay to ride. I'm always impressed by women who've made the decision to ride a motorcycle because I know for most it wasn't easy — whether it was a family member telling them they can't do it or people at their work don't think it's appropriate or they're a mother with small children and they're told they shouldn't ride. I also know motorcycling is not for every woman, that's why those of us who ride have a certain uniqueness to us.

I've discovered over the years that often a woman is going through some kind of a transition when she comes to motorcycling. She may be going through a redefining stage in her life, or she is experiencing a milestone, like turning fifty, or perhaps she's just going through a divorce, or she just became an empty nester. Motorcycling is an extension of that transition. She's figuring out what it means to be a mom with children who don't depend on her daily anymore or she's moving on after being in a dead-end relationship. Motorcycling becomes an expression of those newfound feelings. It also makes a statement about the woman she hopes to become. She's still the same person inside but she's discovering things about herself that she didn't know she had or knew she could do.

Just like climbing a mountain or trying a new sport, motorcycling imparts the same euphoric feelings — feelings that permeate our beings when we've accomplished something monumental in our lives. Riding on the highway for the first time, doing a U-turn without putting our feet down or facing Mother Nature's challenges on a mountaintop — all are significant accomplishments.

I find I face life's challenges head-on rather than approaching them with "I can't," or "I won't" or "I shouldn't." In fact, I was just talking about skiing to a friend yesterday and it really struck me, because she's very successful in business, but she has this self-deprecating attitude about her skiing ability. "I'm not really very good. I go slowly. I'm afraid of heights." It was weird to hear a fifty-year-old woman saying these negative things about herself. It made me reflect on my own abilities and attitude toward challenges. I don't say "I can't" about many things, although I'm better at certain things than others. Motorcycling has created in me a "can do" attitude toward challenges and perceived obstacles in my life.

There really are no barriers for women to riding a motorcycle anymore. The only barriers a woman has are self-imposed. We are in a culture today where stereotypes of women riders and society's views of riders are yesterday's news. You don't need anyone's permission to ride, other than your own. If you can't give yourself permission to get on a bike, then you're not ready. But once you've reached that place in your mind, then you're ready to handle the challenges that come with being a rider. If you really want to do it, you'll do it.

I'm always learning. On a recent trip, I was riding a large touring motorcycle that wasn't my own, and I was particularly exhausted this day after riding five hundred miles. At the end of this very long and arduous day, my riding partner talked me into continuing another eighty miles. It turned out to be eighty miles on a curvy road in deep pre-asphalt gravel, and it was as scary as heck on that big bagger. I had to muster up extra mental fortitude so I could translate that into the physical strength needed because if I had approached this challenge mentally with "I can't do this," then my body would have remained in that fatigue state setting me up for failure. It was an extreme time, and I really had to pull from within to get to where we were going and to do it safely. My intuition was loudly trying to tell me something different than what I ended up doing, but I had already committed to riding those additional miles. Motorcycling is a situation where it's not a good idea to ignore your inner voice, because it could be a life-or-death situation.

I'm really strong in my mind. That's what it takes and that's what I needed at that time. At that moment I was wrestling with how I got talked into riding another eighty miles when I was so fatigued. I became angry. The big lesson for me that day was to not only know my own limitations but to speak up and put my foot down when I hear my inner voice. At the time I was trying to appease my riding partner.

Often when we're in a group ride we're pressured to ride, say, faster than we want. No more. I now go the speed I want. "If you want to go ahead, great," I say. "I'll see you when I get there." But boy oh boy, it's taken many years to get to that point of riding my own ride. I feel badly for women who don't possess the mind power to speak up like that. One major lesson I try to impart in my speeches is that you can stand up for yourself when you're out of your comfort zone. You don't need to wait ten years to figure that out like I did. You have that power now.

Rebecca Herwick

Occupation: president and chief executive officer,
Global Products Inc.
Location: St. Louis, Missouri
Age: 51
Riding Discipline: street
Began Riding: 1966 (mini-bikes); 1981 (first own Harley)
Website: gpii.com

Rebecca's Global Products is a multimillion-dollar organization that brings together her interests of business, motorcycling and giving back to her community. The company is a dealer-exclusive designer, manufacturer and distributor of official, licensed Harley-Davidson® headwear, giftware and collectibles. After a very close friend suffered a debilitating head injury, she became involved in the Center for Head Injury Services and the Brain Injury Association and employs people from the Center. She has also served on the National Women's Business Council, Women's Business Enterprise National Council and the Missouri Head Injury Advisory Council.

We spoke on November 21, 2008. She says a solo motorcycle trip in 1982 had a lot to do with her developing the skills that have gotten her where she is today. Getting out on one of her five Harleys still gives her the ideal opportunity to process her decisions.

My hometown was a farm town with lots of cows and corn. The kids used motorcycles and mini-bikes as transportation between the farms to see each other. I rode the mini-bikes, I rode a boyfriend's motorcycle, and then, when I was in college studying chemistry, I bought a 1976 Harley-Davidson Sportster. It was very unusual for a girl to ride a motorcycle at that time in 1970, just as it was unusual for a girl to get a degree in chemistry.

I was perceived as rebellious. One of the monikers I received in high school was "most likely to go to jail". A lot of people automatically thought motorcycle riders were rebellious, untamed and not following the rules, guidelines and standards. Those assumptions were made, and I kind of enjoyed them. I was a bit rebellious and I didn't mind the assumptions people made. I didn't follow the social rules. I had my own mind and I didn't have a problem with that.

Please note I've never been arrested. I have always followed a moral and ethical compass. I'm a firm believer in societal rights and rules and regulations. It's just that, for me personally, people's perceptions are irrelevant.

I believe every person is a diamond with so many different facets. I can wear an Escada suit today and be in an inappropriate T-shirt tomorrow. It's how you look at me or the day or the time. The face is always Rebecca but I have many facets as an individual.

I had a Super Glide with no windshield and no radio when I rode alone from St. Louis, Missouri, to Sturgis, South Dakota, in mid-July, 1982. I met so many people along the way who were fascinated by this woman who was doing this and they wanted to talk to me. That ride was such a memorable experience — being so comfortable by myself, having the confidence to do it and succeeding in it, having a cable break and being able to fix it, building that relationship with myself, spending that much time alone. That was a long way to go and it wasn't exactly an era where that was a typical behavior. I had no reference points. I didn't know anybody who had already done it. What I gained from it personally in self-confidence is what makes it my most valuable motorcycle ride.

On that ride, I overcame the perception that being alone, doing something individually or accomplishing something on your own is isolation. The path you've gone on creates a crack in the ceiling for other people to do the same thing.

That experience of traveling alone and having a wonderful time with me allows me to do what I'm doing now. I own the company myself. I make the decisions. I don't have a business partner. I live alone and I'm very comfortable with that. That ride in that era hastened my ability to define my character as being able to accomplish something on my own without somebody riding next to me or sitting behind somebody.

Cultivating personal power is very difficult. Even today I have issues where I have to choose to take the back seat because it's best overall. Choosing when to put your decisions first and knowing when to take the back seat cultivates a good leader. You have to look at the impact you have around you, the trail you leave behind from the things you've done. And you have to make sure the net outcome benefits the majority. Sometimes, it's very tough. You have to look forward and back, right and left.

Motorcycling gives me great opportunities for thinking. The more I have processed a strategy, the better that decision is. When I ride, that's when I really get that time. When I ride, it's beautiful and it feels wonderful. I get a sense of empowerment while I'm blind-processing about how I'm going to take control or how I want to move forward or how this will impact me three, five, ten or generationally twenty or forty years from now.

It's important that, when something devastating happens, which it does to all of us, a lot depends on the glasses you have on, how you look at it and how you perceive it. It can either be a tragedy and destroy you or you can work your way through it. Of course, you've got to cry, you've got to yell at God, but then you have to make it into something that benefits other people. That way it's no longer a tragedy. It was important. You were the chosen one. It happened because you needed to do this. If other people can benefit, and many people can benefit from a tragedy, then it's empowering.

I'm not saying it's easy. I don't want to talk about this like it is something everybody should do with every horrible thing that happens in their life. As I was going through it, trust me, I had no idea I was making it into something good. I was just dealing with it day by day. And the next thing I know I have created this environment and was in this environment. It was not premeditated.

I turned around one day and realized where I was standing was a remarkable place and I could do something with it. But I don't want to minimize the difficulty.

I am on the board for the Center for Head Injury Services and I see the brain-injury victims with their family members, so I see the pain in their eyes. But they're working toward legislation, they are working toward charitable events and they are creating better environments for people who are brain injured. So quite a few people have done the same thing as I have done and will continue to do it.

With the sport, I love the fact that it is being shared equally, regardless of gender, and I think that is an indicator of society. The more I see women riding motorcycles, the more I know our society is becoming balanced across the board. And the more women you see on motorcycles, the more women you see in positions of power. At home, at work, at play — I think there's more equality. It isn't just about motorcycles. It's about empowering women.

THE LAST WORD

ONCE UPON A TIME there was a woman who lived a simple life in a small cabin nestled in a dense, vibrant, hardwood forest. She enjoyed adventures, walking in the woods during the day and gazing at the starry heavens at night. Daily, she spent time in contemplation and prayer and although she made a lot of changes in her life trying to do the right thing, she had trouble following her own wisdom and inner guidance. Her mind was very good at making all kinds of noise, which led to worry and made listening difficult and decisions confusing. Mostly the confusion resulted from fear. She was afraid to listen too closely because she'd be guided in a direction that was new to her.

Fear made everything seem foggy, and she couldn't see where she was going. She knew she was on the right path and headed in the right direction, but there were obstacles. Rather than slowing down and letting the noise settle and her vision clear, she blindly kept pushing forward. Eventually, on a spring day, the weight of what she was carrying was too much and her shoulder broke under the load.

God gently spoke to her in that moment. "Stop, sit, and rest for a while in the beautiful woods you love so much." To make sure she stopped and to help her understand her power came from within, God gave her right arm a rest for a while.

While she was sitting on the path in the woods, an angel came by and pointed at the beautiful patch of trilliums growing in the woods where the woman was looking and not seeing. The angel noted, "I've never seen so many trilliums — and they're not behind you; they're only in front of you."

The woman marveled. Trilliums meant new life, growth, energy and the beginning of a new cycle, and she hadn't noticed them until the angel pointed to them in her future. Other angels guided the woman back to her cabin, where she could rest and heal.

The woman knows she still has fears to conquer, but she's recognizing them sooner. They kept her from following her true path and realizing her potential, but now she has only begun to tap into her limitless power. She knows she is guided and cared for, her prayers are always heard and answered and she has no need to be afraid. Many people love her and she is never alone. She is wealthy in many ways and so grateful for the abundance in her life that she must share her learnings with others so they, too, know how to find the treasure.

BIBLIOGRAPHY

1. *Awareness: The Perils and Opportunities of Reality*, Anthony de Mello, Doubleday

2. *Transitions, Making Sense of Life's Changes*, Second Edition, William Bridges, Da Capo Press

3. *Change Your Thoughts — Change Your Life: Living the Wisdom of the Tao*, Dr. Wayne W. Dyer, Hay House Inc.

4. *If Not Now, When?*, Stephanie Marston, Warner Books

5. *Invisible Acts of Power: Personal Choices That Create Miracles*, Carolyn Myss, Ph.D., Free Press

6. *Life Lessons for Women*, Jack Canfield, Mark Victor Hansen and Stephanie Marston, Health Communications Inc.

7. *Mennonites, Politics, and Peoplehood*, James Urry, University of Manitoba Press

8. *Spiritual Literacy: Reading the Sacred in Everyday Life*, Frederic and Mary Ann Brussat, Simon and Shuster

9. *The Biology of Belief: Unleashing the Power of Consciousness, Matter and Miracles*, Bruce H. Lipton, Ph.D., Mountain of Love/Elite Books

10. *The Four Agreements*, Don Miguel Ruiz, M.D., Amber-Allen Publishing

11. *The Hero With a Thousand Faces*, Joseph Campbell, Princeton University Press

12. *The Path of Least Resistance: Learning to Become the Creative Force in Your Own Life,* Robert Fritz, Faucet Columbine

13. *The Seven Mysteries of Life: An Exploration of Science and Philosophy,* Guy Murchie, Houghton, Mifflin Company

14. *The Women Who Broke All the Rules: How the Choices of a Generation Changed Our Lives,* Susan B. Evans, Joan P. Avis, Sourcebooks Inc.

15. *The Spontaneous Healing of Belief: Shattering the Paradigm of False Limits,* Gregg Braden, Hay House Inc.

16. *Why People Don't Heal and How They Can,* Caroline Myss, Ph.D., Three Rivers Press

17. *Women Who Run With the Wolves,* Clarissa Pinkola Estés, Ph.D., Ballantine Books

About the Author

LIZ JANSEN is an entrepreneur, adventurer, writer — and rider extraordinaire.

She creates motorcycle experiences that instill a sense of adventure, freedom and community while traveling the transformative road to personal and professional leadership. Liz has worked with individuals, corporate clients, manufacturers, retailers and the public sector.

Made in the USA
San Bernardino, CA
24 October 2012